Praise for *Audacious Optimism*

"*Shanna's outlook on optimism is a powerful message for patients or anyone going through challenging times. Her bravery in the face of adversity and her determination to maintain hope despite life's obstacles is an inspiring reminder of the power of mental strength.*"

—Douglas Anderson, MD
Professor of Neurosurgery, Loyola University Medical Center

"*My connection with Shanna goes far beyond her health journey. She has always exuded a strong sense of hope, and I knew she would face her diagnosis and recovery with that same determination. I will always remember the first picture she sent me, with her beaming smile during the crucial first weeks of her recovery. I thought to myself, she's truly remarkable—hope is an invaluable resource for any patient.*"

—Amy L. Pittman, MD
Associate Professor, Department of Otolaryngology Head &
Neck Surgery, Loyola University Medical Center

"*In her book* Audacious Optimism, *Shanna uses her inspiring storytelling to ignite a fire within us. She is an extraordinary woman—someone whose beauty radiates not just from her outward appearance but from the depths of her spirit. Her powerful message of audacious optimism and self-assurance struck a chord with me. I have witnessed firsthand how she harnesses optimism to accomplish great things in her life. Her words serve as a guide for anyone seeking a strong and authentic dose of motivation and inspiration.*"

—Jeanette Prenger
Founder and CEO of ECCO Select

Audacious

Optimism

SHANNA ADAMIC

Audacious

Optimism

**THE MINDFUL CHOICE TO LIVE BOLDLY
AND CREATE ENDLESS POSSIBILITIES**

WILEY

Published by John Wiley & Sons, Inc., Hoboken, New Jersey.
Published simultaneously in Canada.

For general information on our other products and services or for technical support, please contact our Customer Care Department within the United States at (800) 762-2974, outside the United States at (317) 572-3993, or fax (317) 572-4002.

Wiley also publishes its books in a variety of electronic formats. Some content that appears in print may not be available in electronic formats. For more information about Wiley products, visit our web site at www.wiley.com.

Library of Congress Cataloging-in-Publication Data

Names: Adamic, Shanna, author.
Title: Audacious optimism : the mindful choice to live boldly and create
  endless possibilities / Shanna Adamic.
Description: Hoboken, New Jersey : John Wiley & Sons, Inc., 2025.
Identifiers: LCCN 2024029660 (print) | LCCN 2024029661 (ebook) | ISBN
  9781394289677 (hardback) | ISBN 9781394289691 (adobe pdf) | ISBN
  9781394289684 (epub)
Subjects: LCSH: Adamic, Shanna. | Brain—Tumors—Patients—United
  States—Biography. | Philanthropists—United States—Biography. |
  Optimism.
Classification: LCC RC280.B7 A25 2025 (print) | LCC RC280.B7 (ebook) |
  DDC 616.99/4810092 [B]—dc23/eng/20240802
LC record available at https://lccn.loc.gov/2024029660
LC ebook record available at https://lccn.loc.gov/2024029661

Cover Design: Paul McCarthy
Cover Photograph: Courtesy of the Author

Mom: *Thank you for your love, and for reading me*
My Turn On Earth.

Dad: *Thank you for loving me. You'll always be my hero.*

Krissy: *You left us too soon, sweet friend. With joy forever.*

Contents

Introduction

Imagine a simple smile transforming your day and potentially changing your entire life.

When someone directs a warm and genuine smile toward you, it's almost impossible not to return the gesture because they are contagious. Yes, contagious, which means you naturally will smile back, if you let yourself.

In fact, when we choose to smile back at someone or even at ourselves in the mirror, our brains release endorphins and serotonin—two powerful ingredients that ignite feelings of happiness and reduce stress. A genuine smile has the power to instantly shift our mindset, infuse hope into our thoughts, and boost our confidence all because we made the choice to smile—a choice deeply rooted in optimism.

Optimism is an incredible force that resides within each one of us. It's a power that we can tap into and utilize every single day, affecting our interactions with others, shaping our experiences, and ultimately influencing our outcomes. The key is making the mindful choice to harness this power, and sometimes the spark of optimism can be lit by the simple yet powerful act of smiling.

Go ahead and try it—smile.

My Journey

I grew up in small-town Liberty, Missouri, in the 1980s, ready for action, set on finding adventure, and filled with youthful joy. Double braids in my hair and a huge smile on my face, I had big dreams and plans to accomplish every single one of them. I believed I could do anything and be anyone.

There was a certain magic to the wild innocence of those days—the warm summers spent pedaling bikes for hours, leaving them in a neighbor's yard before running off with friends to the nearby park. The thrill of climbing over fences and taking leaps into an aboveground pool filled every moment with excitement. And after a long day of playing, I'd return home to a welcoming house, surrounded by the scent of freshly cut grass, where the sound of the attic fan echoed through the halls and provided relief from the scorching summer heat.

Every time I close my eyes in the summer, the sound comes rushing back as if it were yesterday. It captures the long, hot days spent picking juicy tomatoes from my mom's garden, watching my dad expertly grill burgers. The humming of the attic fan was more than just a sound—it was a feeling of love, comfort, and family enveloping me in its gentle embrace. As the seasons shifted, the warmth of the open windows welcomed in the cool, crisp breeze of fall, carrying with it the anticipation and excitement of Christmas.

As the holiday season approached, I looked forward to wearing cozy pajamas with my older brothers by my side and watching the movie *A Christmas Story*. The warmth of the fireplace felt comforting as we lay on the floor in front of the TV covered with a blanket right by our beautifully decorated tree. It was a magical time in our lives, until Christmas of 1989 when everything changed. That was the year my father lost his battle against leukemia and lymphoma after months of fighting at the VA hospital. I was just nine years old.

A few days before he died, my mom took us to see him. As I walked into the hospital, I was scared. Everything felt sad, looked brown, smelled sterile, and sounded like incessant beeping. I didn't want my daddy to be there; I wanted him home with us, healthy and not hooked up to machines.

When is Daddy going to come home? I thought to myself as we turned the corner to his room. I will never forget the image of him sitting on the side of his bed—a navy robe wrapped around his painfully thin body, his head hung low, and his brown skin sagging from his face—holding a medical IV pole. My dad had always been full of life, with a huge personality to match and a laugh that could pour sunshine into any dark room. Now the cancer had made him almost unrecognizable to me.

My mom and brothers walked in and hugged him. I slid through the door and sat quietly at the end of the uncomfortable hospital bed, listening to them talk. I just stared at my dad, taking in every feature while the noise around me sounded like the indecipherable adults in the Charlie Brown cartoons. My body was buzzing with a nervous energy that I didn't understand.

My dad stared into my eyes with a mixture of love and sadness. With a weak smile, he reached out and placed his hand on mine. In that moment, I felt an overwhelming sense of comfort and security. "I love you," he said, his voice filled with emotion. My face lit up with a smile, and I said, "I love you too, Daddy!" And then, with a soft chuckle and a wide grin revealing his imperfect teeth, he leaned over and whispered, "Never stop smiling."

His infectious charm and larger-than-life personality were like medicine for my soul. I held onto his every word, not wanting to let go of this perfect moment. Though life is fleeting, and he was taken from us far too soon.

The memory of my dad's words in that hospital room has never left me, and each morning I greet the day and myself with a determined smile. However, as someone who spent years dancing on the sidelines for the National Football League (NFL) as a professional cheerleader, I can attest that life is not just about flashy touchdown celebrations or big wins. Life is a complex dance of the highest highs and the lowest lows, and sometimes those smiles don't come easily.

Life is wonderful, but hard. It's about how you pick yourself up when you're down, how you dance through defeat, how you smile despite how impossible or daunting the moment might feel for finding an ember of hope in such dark moments. That's the true mark of a champion. My champion spirit was refined with my life experiences and polished as a professional athlete with the Kansas City Chiefs—when the clock is running out and hope seems lost, that's when you need a cheerleader spirit the most. It's about igniting that spark, rallying the crowd, and turning the game around against all odds.

We might not all have a squad or pom-poms on standby for tough times, but we've got something even more powerful: the ability to rally from within. It's the power to choose optimism, which at times, can start with a simple smile, harnessing our inner cheerleader to push through fear and stand tall when the stakes and odds of failure are both high. It's facing challenges with a calm, resilient spirit, and a will that's patient yet unyielding.

This is audacious optimism—bold hope and confidence in the future. While I didn't know it at the time, this spirit lived in me decades ago.

Financial struggles hit hard after my dad passed; my parents had poured their paychecks and my mom had poured her support into his years of doctor appointments, failed treatments, and gaps in insurance coverage. We relied on the generosity of our church's pantry at times just to get by. We were also blessed with an incredible extended family who stepped in when we needed it most.

My mom was my first example of audacious optimism. After my father's passing, she fought tooth and nail to keep our lives as enchanting as they had always been. Even if her personality didn't outwardly project strength and she herself didn't feel it—I saw it. She found a way to push past the doubt and fear and seek opportunity in the darkness even if only for the sake of loving her kids.

I've always actively searched for the opportunity in every obstacle. I have lived a life full of many privileges and many challenges—facing difficult struggles and experiencing loss. Through it all, I have persevered and emerged stronger. I have also soared, fueled by my intentional and mindful choice to live life as an optimist and fight for my smile to take form in the face of adversity.

Even today, I choose to see opportunity with confidence when the way ahead looks dark. My cup, though at times it feels as if it might slip from my hand and shatter, has never been half empty. Even in those moments where I almost lost my grip, it has always been full of possibility and potential. My optimism is bold and empowers me to make positive change and envision a better future with hope and confidence.

Audacious optimism is my North Star, illuminating the path ahead as I face every challenge with determination. It serves as a constant reminder of the boundless power in making a mindful choice, trusting myself, having the courage to stay curious and embrace the unknown, tapping into my mental toughness by declaring, "I will," and taking bold steps toward what once seemed impossible.

This philosophy isn't just a one-time decision, but a daily practice of small, positive actions that ultimately lead to profound results. It became my lifeline during the most trying time of my life—battling a life-threatening brain tumor—and continues to guide me through every challenge that will come.

From 2011 to 2017, I engaged with my primary care physician (PCP), various specialists, and multiple hospitals 109 times. One hundred and nine times. The average woman in her 30s sees a doctor just a few times per year. My health was spiraling, and I could not figure out why. The journey to a credible diagnosis was long, and the road was rocky. It nearly broke my belief and trust in myself—my instinct, my voice. I felt crazy. I felt weak. I sought answers for a problem that doctors assured and reassured me was not there.

After being misdiagnosed, underdiagnosed, underinformed, given lifestyle advice connected with being a woman, and written off with symptoms of being a tired working mom, I finally received the answer I needed. I was diagnosed with a rare, life-threatening, though benign, brain tumor. It was the answer I needed, not the one I expected or wanted at all.

When that life-altering diagnosis finally came, my self-trust rushed back through my body like water bursting through a dam. I was also overwhelmed with the terrifying knowledge and uncertainty of what I would face. It took me six years to get to this point, and I was not letting six more years go by before I had the right care plan in place. Truth is, I didn't have six years—I had one. One year.

Over the course of my health care journey, what I felt the health care professionals saw each time I sought medical attention on the outside was a healthy and high-functioning female. However, what they couldn't see on the inside was that I was begging for intelligent and connected care that could identify the problem my body knew was there. I had to learn and relearn how to be my own advocate and press the doctors to pay attention to my symptoms. I needed to share my entire journey and story—struggling to raise my voice when I began feeling defeated along the way.

I had to dig deep to find a single ember of hope in total darkness. Not only was I physically struggling with headaches, hearing loss, speech complications, and loss of balance, but I was also mentally and emotionally spent. I questioned and doubted myself, wondering whether I was overreacting or making things up. It was in those moments I had to learn to choose audacity over defeat, determination over uncertainty. I knew what I felt, and what I felt wasn't normal.

My prognosis was a one-year life expectancy without the right surgery and care plan. The first care plan I discussed with doctors after my diagnosis included multiple surgeries and radiation—for me personally, this didn't offer much hope. My instincts kicked in and I exercised my right as a patient knowing I needed a second opinion, and I needed it fast. Frantically, I contacted other doctors and hospitals, and they wouldn't schedule me without a referral. Getting a second opinion on my own was impossible. I turned to social media—a modern marvel that became a beacon of hope. I shared my story, and within hours I had a glimmer. A response came from an old college friend, now a physician and surgeon, who ended up working with the team of doctors addressing my specific tumor.

Before long, I found myself connected with a team in Chicago, Illinois, whose second opinion included a big surgery and a tough recovery, but a promising outcome. This was my chance to take back my life! It also meant leaving behind the familiar comfort of my local care and community of support, but I was determined to do whatever it took to ensure that my body, brain, and future were in the right hands.

Thankfully, I had the resources and support I needed to make this journey possible—a barrier that needs to be removed for every person. Determined, I made all necessary arrangements to entrust my health and well-being to this new team of experts.

Embarking on a journey to find care and undergo surgery was a leap into the unknown, far from a guaranteed win. My optimism was tested, and that light almost went dark.

Looking back on my journey and my dad's battle, I recognize too many similarities. Three decades later, and, like my mom, I had to navigate the winding, confusing, and unfair US health care system. Maybe my father would have survived with an early diagnosis, the right care plan, digitized and connected health care, and the financial backing that would have given him access to necessary resources. As a child, I held tight to my father as he fought hard, battling a disease against all odds, and I watched my mom struggle to get him the care he deserved.

Sadly, we are not the only family who has gotten lost in the maze of health care. The system is full of noise: the rapid speed of digital innovation, the systemic bias causing mis- and missed diagnoses, the unequal and nonexistent access to dignified care, the endless demand on doctors to see hundreds of patients, and the slow disappearance of the lifelong family practitioner. There's so much beeping, so many hallways, and too many closed doors. Optimism in health care can sometimes feel impossible for patients and providers, yet it is essential for healing. We need hope for our future and confidence and belief in humanity in health care.

After college, I joined a company that was working to transform health care by digitizing the medical records to eliminate waste, error, variance, and delay. It instilled in me that health care is personal and too important to stay the same. As a part of the charitable pediatric foundation First Hand Foundation I launched my serendipitously fateful philanthropy career, leading the charge to remove financial barriers to essential health care for children around the world.

I never imagined experiencing the depths of health care as personally as I have, at least not so young. Thankfully, my professional and personal experiences provided the source of knowledge and power I needed in 2017 to find the right approach, plan, and team to restore my normal life—as a woman, wife, mother, sister, friend, and colleague.

That's why in 2018, I underwent a nearly 13-hour translaby-rinthine craniotomy to remove the tumor. My second opinion gave me my second chance at life.

My recovery from brain surgery was brutal. Instead of cheering for a football team, I had to become my own cheerleader and encourage myself. I had to become an active participant in my own recovery and accept, appreciate, and love the parts of me that had changed. I had to lean into optimism as a choice that many times felt gritty and hard. I needed audacious optimism to love myself and take back my life.

Many times, I had to fight to tap into my mental toughness by telling myself, *I will heal. I will put one foot in front of the other. I will face the frail woman staring back at me in the mirror and love her deeply.* The power of optimism in those moments fueled my soul. I had been right that something was wrong, and experts had missed it; now there was no one I trusted more than myself. I let my renewed self-trust fill me with the confidence that I would come out of this challenge as a stronger version of myself and determined to make a change for others.

While on a slow and grueling recovery journey, I made progress. To keep going, I made a list of seemingly simple goals and placed it on that bathroom mirror where, daily, I faced an unfamiliar and worn-down woman staring back at me:

I will smile with all my teeth.
I will close my right eye completely.
I will chew on both sides of my mouth.
I will regain my balance.
I will be a better version of me.

To others, these goals might seem modest, but for me, they were monumental. I recited them daily, a mantra to keep me focused and determined. Each day was a testament to the strength of my mindset over my pain and frailty. Even in the darkest times of my health journey, I never imagined hearing my own voice as clearly as I do today. I wasn't going to allow my pain to become a heavy weighted backpack through my life. No, my pain was going to push me closer to my purpose, and it started with "I will." There is immense power in saying, "I will."

At the beginning, doctors had given me a mere 4% chance of regaining my smile. Today, I'm thrilled to share that I defied those odds, and my cheeky smile has made a full comeback—and I know my dad is smiling right back at me!

It was a miraculous transformation, one that I could hardly believe at first. I was truly living, seeing, and understanding the power of resilience and determination. I had faced the most difficult battle of my life and pushed through it. Asking the hard questions and facing my deepest fears were essential parts of the journey. The weight of them sat heavy on my chest, threatening to suffocate me. When I put pen to paper and wrote them down, a sense of clarity washed over me. I could see each fear for what it truly was: a challenge to be overcome, not a barrier to hold me back. The act of confronting them head-on was empowering.

And with each passing day, I felt myself growing stronger physically and mentally. As I looked in the mirror, I no longer saw a weak, terrified stranger. I saw someone who had overcome incredible odds and emerged stronger because of it. I saw my smile.

For me, it was a journey of sheer will, a battle fought with the strength of hope and a champion spirit.

Facing this unimaginable health journey challenged my approach to optimism and taught me the profound power of a mindful choice.

It's about standing toe to toe with your deepest fears and choosing to see beyond them. It's about recognizing that fear is nothing more than a challenge to be met with courage and curiosity. When confronted, the fear diminishes, and all that's left is your true potential.

This newfound strength isn't just a fleeting feeling; it's a transformative force. It's the kind of optimism that shatters ceilings and redefines boundaries. It's what kept me standing, cheering, and looking forward with hope, a smile on my face, even when life gave me its worst.

Your Journey

Dear reader, if there is one thing you take from this book it is that your mind is a powerful force. Let it choose optimism, even in the darkest of times. Let it open your eyes to opportunities where others, yourself included, may see only obstacles. Let it give you courage—the kind that knows no limits as you face challenges head-on, curious and eager to learn and unafraid to fail. And above all, let it make you bold enough to never give up on yourself, constantly showing up for yourself with unshakable determination.

So what is the recipe for audacious optimism? Great question! There are four elements. I say elements intentionally, because they are all essential ingredients, and it begins with **a mindful choice**. Our choices are mirrors of our true selves. They showcase what we value, what we want, and what we prioritize. When we choose to be kind instead of resentful or brave instead of afraid, we shape our identity. Optimism is found in the power of choice—it is not a passive feeling. Choosing optimism is understanding that we can shape ourselves, every single step, response and outcome, through the hopeful and confident decisions we make.

When choosing to approach life with optimism you automatically step into the next element: **trust yourself**. Trust your inner voice, the one that rings loud and clear in your mind and heart, urging you to act and speak your truth. Your instinct. Your gut feeling. When you silence this voice, you conform to societal expectations, miss out on opportunities, partnerships, and relationships, and limit your potential for growth and happiness.

The third element is to **embrace the unknown**. At times, it may be uncomfortable and frightening, but it also holds endless possibilities. The unknown can evoke fear and doubt, and it is ever-present on the journey to achieving our dreams. We must accept that we don't know what lies ahead. We must stay curious and have faith that there is always opportunity even if we can only see one step at a time. Take a deep breath in and exhale out, step forward, and bravely face the unknown.

The fourth element is **mental toughness**. This is the quality of being able to remain strong and determined when facing challenges. It goes beyond just being resilient; it is a refusal to give up even when the odds seem insurmountable. Mental toughness is refined when you remove words such as "should," "could," and "would" from your vocabulary, fearlessly declaring instead, "*I will!*" Speak your vision for the future as if it is already yours. When we declare confidently that we will achieve something, we are claiming our future. This powerful statement propels us forward and sets things in motion. Remember, this is not just for individuals. Leaders can adopt this mental toughness as a strategy for success for their team or company culture, by changing "I will" to "we will"—fostering a sense of unity and shared resilience and determination.

When all of these elements are practiced—mindful choice, trust yourself, embrace the unknown, and mental toughness—**the**

seemingly impossible can happen. When we first align our thoughts with hopeful and confident determination, what seemed out of reach now feels attainable. It all starts with *you*, your mind, and the power to transform your thoughts so they're filled with opportunity, hope, and belief in your future.

Let me also be clear on what audacious optimism is not. It is not just a fleeting thought or an occasional feeling—it is bold, mindful, deliberate.

Optimism cannot be passively waited for; it must be actively chosen. It's not a feeling or emotion. It's not something you can wait for or expect to just happen to you. It's a mindful decision, one that we must make every day and in every situation. We all have natural tendencies toward positivity or negativity, but at the end of the day, optimism is a choice that anyone can make at any time.

Optimism is also not synonymous with positivity or happiness. While they are important and can fuel optimism, they too are rooted in emotion and can sometimes serve as a toxic excuse for denying less-than-ideal situations. In fact, the pressure to appear "positive" or "fine" all the time will hinder a genuine response and emotional experience. This leads to overwhelming and internalized stress and emotional suppression.[1] Optimism can be chosen even without initial feelings of positivity because it is a conscious decision rather than an emotion.

Similarly, happiness may be seen as the end goal of choosing optimism, but it is not interchangeable with optimism. Happiness is temporary and finite, while optimism can continually cultivate joy and contentment. Use optimism as a tool to achieve happiness, but don't confuse the two concepts.

As I have said, this has become my anchor, my daily practice, and my life strategy. This practice for me starts every day at 6 a.m. when my alarm goes off. The first thing I do is get up from my bed without hitting snooze—a small and powerful act of determination. I make my way to the bathroom. There, I look at myself in the mirror and smile—yes, I smile at my half-awake and hair-not-brushed self. This is a simple action that can completely transform my mood because it creates a spark of joy and hope. It may seem insignificant, but smiling at yourself is where optimism can take form.

Next, whether in the shower, walking my dog, preparing my morning coffee, or, if time allows, on the yoga mat, I take intentional deep breaths, inhaling stress, doubt, or fears that may be lingering in my mind from yesterday's stress or today's agenda and exhaling strength and confidence. For me, box breathing, also known as square breathing, is the method I choose because it is perfect for combating stress.[2] But regardless of whether the time or place allows for a formal breathing exercise, I just take a simple breath and release it. This simple practice helps me ground myself and set the right tone for the day ahead, one that I can repeat throughout the day if needed. I also find that it allows me to take a moment to be grateful for the gifts in my life. Now, sometimes it is tough to be grateful when life has kicked you in the heart, or the kids have been crazy and I haven't slept, yet this is the moment I need gratitude the most. I find myself, many times, just being thankful for the hot coffee in my hands, and that is a great gift!

Perhaps the most powerful action I take daily to cultivate optimism is my own mental toughness and repeating those two words that I love and, hopefully, have hammered into your brain by now: "I will." Whether I write it on bright pink Post-it notes scattered across my desk, type it into my phone's notes app, or say it out loud to myself, every method works. It serves as a powerful affirmation that I am capable and determined to accomplish whatever comes my way, big or small: I will make that call, I will do my laundry, I will make it to the gym. It states my intention. Saying "I will" encourages you to commit to your personal power. It is well known that regularly proclaiming intention can align your daily actions with your broader life goals, encouraging you to take action toward your big dreams.

By incorporating a daily practice of optimism into your life, you become more than just an individual—you become an inspiration for those around you. You can turn ambitious dreams into tangible actions and propel yourself and your team—whether at home or work—forward. In the face of adversity, you become a seeker of opportunity and a source of light that brightens every space you enter. You are the ultimate cheerleader, lifting spirits even when faced with impossible odds. With the power of optimism by your side, you can bring about meaningful change for yourself and others.

Choosing optimism is a conscious decision, requiring mindful intentionality. It's about taking small, consistent steps that anchor each day and cultivate the mindset needed to choose, envision and build a brighter future. Like I said, these practices have become my lifeline, and I am eager to share them with you through my personal story.

I invite you to join the ranks of audacious optimists and take control of your own story. This is my intimate tale of how optimism has shaped my life, which I want to share with all of you. Next, I invite you to tell your story and passion for optimism with me at http://audaciousoptimism.com on the Share Your Optimism page.

Thank you for allowing me to share small parts of my life, heart, and health journey with you.

In the words of my dad, "Never stop smiling."

Notes

1. https://nexus.jefferson.edu/health/can-too-much-positivity-be-a-negative
2. https://www.verywellhealth.com/breathing-techniques-8382890

A Mindful Choice

Choice is the cornerstone of human existence, an omnipresent force that guides your journey and shapes your identity. The power of choice gives you agency in life, empowering you to take control of your circumstances and navigate through life's tumultuous waters. It grants you the ability to assert your autonomy and make decisions that align with your values, desires, and dreams. Each choice you make reveals a part of who you are as an individual, capturing your unique preferences, beliefs, and priorities within its delicate folds.

With choice also comes consequence—each decision, no matter how big or small, carries the weight of impact not just on yourself, but on those around you. You must bear the responsibility for these outcomes, whether they be positive or negative. For it is ultimately your choices that guide you down new paths, filled with experiences that mold you into the person you are meant to become. Like painters on a blank canvas, you hold the brush of free will in your hands.

In the end, it is your choices that intricately weave together the fabric of your existence, influence the relationships you form, and define your journey. And when you come to understand that you have a choice in every situation—even amid an unpredictable and sometimes impossible world—you also come to realize that choosing optimism is an audacious act of bravery and trust.

The Fall

There are moments that pierce through the fabric of our existence, disrupting the natural flow of space and time. These
moments hold such weight and shock that we can pinpoint the
single second our lives forever change, whether it be a world
event such as 9/11 or the announcement of a global pandemic, a
serious accident, an abrupt end to a relationship, losing a job, or
worse, a loved one, or receiving a life-altering diagnosis. In those
moments of interruption, there is a clear division between before
and after. The world seems to shift on its axis, leaving us grasping
for stability—frozen. In the midst of this upheaval, it is easy to
feel uprooted and powerless. It's easy to give up the power that is
choosing optimism.

Everyone has experienced these moments, and it may feel as
though your choice has been taken from you. But the truth is,
you always have a choice. You choose how to keep living, how to
respond, and how to navigate a new reality. You can't change
what happened, but you have control over what you do next—
how you choose to move forward and shape your own story.

For me, this moment came as summer turned into fall in 2017.

August 2017: Whispers Within

My husband, Jeff, and I had some trips planned for the fall, and
our first was to Oregon for my longtime best friend Laura's wedding. I couldn't wait to go! She had talked about how beautiful it
was in the Pacific Northwest, and we needed a vacation. This
sounded perfect.

We decided to stay at the historic Columbia Gorge Hotel &
Spa that overlooked the Hood River. It is breathtaking and con-
sistently windy, attracting windsurfers from around the world.

The car ride to the hotel made me sick to my stomach. The
road wasn't perfectly straight, and by that time any curve in the

road led to me throwing up. Roundabouts were like roller coasters, so I always had a bag with me just in case. Whenever I would see a roundabout coming, I would brace myself, and Jeff would say, "Babe, just calm down. I think you are working yourself up over nothing." I'd give him a side eye. When someone doesn't know what getting motion sickness over the tiniest movement feels like, they don't know that you could vomit everywhere at any minute and there is no control or calming down. He deserved that side eye.

The hotel was captivating! I am a geek for beautifully restored buildings, and this was right up there with the best I had ever seen. It had the romance of the past and the stories each guest left behind. The Italian design influence and the dramatic landscape surrounding it made the place extremely inviting. I sighed. I was so happy not to be driving any longer and to be able to rest for just a few days in this haven of history.

When we got to the room, I looked out from our balcony at the water. The waves were high, crashing against each other, breaking apart only to build up again. It looked dangerous, and I couldn't take my eyes off them. I felt almost sad as I stared at the water. *This is what it feels like in my head. Like turbulent waves crashing and releasing only to form again.*

The trip started with a few days of activities leading up to the wedding: picnicking with the wedding party, visiting town, sipping Oregon wine at the vineyard, and taking in all the beautiful sights.

We had some free time on the third day and decided to take an adventurous hike. Jeff and I probably had a false sense of self at that time, because we told the concierge that we were very athletic and could handle a challenge. Now, what we really needed was a walk up a scenic hill, not the challenging and dense climb we were sent on. We have since learned to come to terms with our level of athleticism.

We knew just a few minutes into our intense hike that it was probably too much for us, but once we start something we press onward and upward. We had to continue up. If I tried to turn my head to look through the trees while we walked, I would get dizzy and feel that I couldn't focus. I stopped several times to close my eyes and correct myself, slowing our pace and likely annoying Jeff. The higher we went, the worse it became, but we kept pushing on. I assumed the dizziness was from my minor fear of heights.

About an hour into the climb, I told Jeff that I was hearing something in the trees, almost as if something were following us. He, of course, like many husbands, thought I was overreacting, and it was probably just in my head. *Apparently, everything was in my head these days.* Still, a buzz was pulsating through my body; there was something with us. I just knew it.

We got to the top of the mountain and took a lovely picture—a picture where I felt I was going to pass out, not from fatigue but from my head spinning. *Was the mountain moving, or were those the waves in my head?* I wondered.

I even asked Jeff whether he felt as if the ground were shifting slightly. He told me the height was probably getting to me, which it was.

I tried to peer over the ledge, just for the experience of viewing the world from that vantage point and immediately pulled back, sitting down to catch my breath. Something about this whole experience was disorienting—the dizziness, the feeling that something was there but unseen. It all made me feel as if I could topple right off the ledge into nothingness. Just falling, and falling, and falling. I was spooked.

We started making our way down the mountain that had taken us a few hours to climb, and every step felt like the slow and steady pace of a grandfather clock—complete with the ominous pendulum sound. We hoped the way down would be faster, but with the loose rocks and cliff's edge that wasn't in the cards.

We were more than halfway down when we saw a legit hiker (who looked a lot more experienced than us) with his golden retriever coming up the same path. The dog came to greet me, wagging its tail like the happy dog that I'm sure it was, and then suddenly stopped to look around. The dog made a little impatient sound and started to nudge me back behind him. I laughed a little and said, "Aren't you the cutest thing?"

The hiker and my husband were standing behind me and had started an easy conversation. This felt normal. I was petting a dog. Jeff was making a new friend. I thought to myself, *See, this is fine, Shanna. Nothing is wrong.*

Then Jeff and the hiker stopped talking mid-sentence.

I had thought the dog's nudging was cute. Well, the dog wasn't trying to be cute. He was trying to herd me away from the *something* I had feared was there all along.

Jeff very calmly said, "Shanna. Stop. Moving."

I stood straight up, still keeping a hand near the dog, looked back at him, and said, "What?" almost a hint of sarcasm in my voice.

He said, again very calmly and slowly, "There is a black bear in front of you."

I snapped my head forward to the path ahead and froze, sucking in one final breath of air before not breathing for what felt like minutes. Brown eyes stared curiously back at me from a fuzzy medium-sized black bear on all fours. Not a cub, but also not quite an adult.

I have heard in these moments you are supposed to stay as still as possible and try not to startle the bear, which is exactly what Jeff, the hiker, and the dog were doing expertly. Not me. That's exactly what I did not do.

My fight, flight, or freeze response jumbled, and I unfroze and immediately switched on flight mode. It took me four long strides and about two seconds to run back up the path and stand behind Jeff and the hiker with the dog at the helm. We all stood there looking like wax museum figures staring at the bear, and the bear continued to stare back at us. I stole a glimpse to each side, trying to find a way out. Jeff felt my movement and said, while keeping his eyes locked on the bear, "Just keep your eyes ahead."

Then the bear did a playful one-two pounce forward and ran back into the dense forest. The hiker then turned to us. "I would move on quickly, because that bear looked young, and I am assuming there is a mom close by."

He didn't have to tell me twice. Jeff and I ran down that trail all the way to the car, not giving notice to any of the scrapes we were getting along the path from our erratic downhill sprint. When we finally got to the car, we jumped in and locked the doors. My legs were shaking. I was out of breath, the pain in the back of my head was pulsating, and my body was buzzing.

Jeff and I looked at each other slowly as we panted for air and started laughing. I started to choke out the laughter as it mixed with crying happy tears. Jeff was doing the same. As he tipped his head back trying to control the hysteria, he barely got out the words, "Well, I guess when you ran back behind me you either wanted me to fight the bear, or you wanted it to have the best chance of eating me first."

We both started laughing so hard our stomachs were cramping and I told him that the kids needed *me* more if one of us had to live. Now, that is not true at all. In fact, he would probably be the better single parent, but the comment made us laugh all the same. Our laughing slowed down, and we let out a big sigh in unison.

"I cannot believe that happened," I said, incredulous at what I was about to say.

"I knew. I mean I *knew*, Jeff. I knew the entire time that something was there. My body felt it!"

He turned on the car as he shook his head in disbelief. "It's crazy, babe. I was just going to say the same thing. You did know, and you tried to tell me. I wonder how long it was there. . . just following us."

A chill went up my body, and I shuddered thinking about it. *How did I know it was there the whole time?* I thought. My body had buzzed at the warning signs. As I replayed every moment in my head, the entire experience began to feel like a slow buildup into an epic thriller.

That evening we had both fallen asleep fast, and I woke up sometime during the middle of the night. The back of my head was throbbing again as if someone had hit me with a baseball bat. I got up to fill a glass with water, hoping that sipping on some would help. *I have to stay hydrated,* I thought. *That's what every doctor has said.*

I took my full glass of water and sat on the side of the bed. As I looked out the balcony door over the Hood River, my body buzzed. It was the same feeling I'd had on the hike. Something was there looming in the shadows of my life, following me. I didn't know what it was, but it was there, just out of sight.

I took a drink and pictured the bear, staring right at me.

I knew you were there the whole time.

September 2017: Losing a Word

Minus the bear encounter, Oregon was a fantastic trip, and I was happy to get home to my babies. Not long after, Jeff surprised me with a trip to Sonoma wine country to celebrate our five-year anniversary. I was thrilled! I had never been.

The morning we were leaving I experienced a relentless wave of vertigo, making me stumble as I tried to pack our bags. I silently blamed the stress of leaving the kids again for this common and exhausting pattern—ignoring any signs or symptoms until they simply fade away.

Despite this, as we drove to the airport and I tried to steady my spinning head, I was looking forward to the trip—if only for the chance to escape and recharge. During the flight, I drifted off into a deep sleep, my head resting comfortably on Jeff's shoulder. He had taken out his tablet and was watching *The Today Show*, one of the in-flight options. Suddenly, he nudged me awake and asked me to watch an interview called "The Fight for Her Life" featuring Savannah Guthrie and Maria Menounos. As I listened to Maria's battle with a brain tumor diagnosis unfold, it struck a chord deep within me, stirring up emotions that I had suppressed—it was both inspiring and terrifying.

In the interview, Maria told Savannah about her brain tumor and the surgery to remove it, as well as her mother's aggressive brain tumor diagnosis. She talked about her problems with chewing and stiffness after the surgery and about the symptoms that led her to talk to her doctors—headaches, fatigue, dizziness.

Jeff turned to me and said, "Wow, those symptoms sound just like some of yours."

Chills ran through my body, almost as if the alarm my body had been ringing became louder, shooting fireworks, sending up smoke flares to get my attention. We got off the plane, and I immediately called my primary care doctor's office, explaining the interview that I had just seen to the nurse. I asked them to refer me to a specialist.

My doctor's office sent over the referral, and I called to schedule an appointment on our way to the resort in Sonoma. After I made the appointment, I decided to just set it and forget it. I knew something was wrong, but a brain tumor seemed too big to consider. *That happens, but surely not to me because we would have known it by now.*

We had an incredible time in Sonoma tasting the wine, enjoying each other's company, and, for me, falling asleep at seven every night. Not kidding, every single night. Jeff told me he had abundant unexpected alone time on the trip because I was always asleep. As all parents of small kids can relate, any moment alone is a moment to sleep. For me, it was more than that, though; I physically couldn't keep my eyes open.

On our trip home, I got a call that I will never forget. The founder of the corporate foundation I worked for had died. Jeanne Lillig-Patterson was a leader, mentor, and my friend. She was someone who could inspire and intimidate anyone with her confidence, passion, and her bold and blunt personality. I loved her. For several years she had struggled with breast cancer that metastasized to her bones and brain. She was tough. She was determined. She was resilient. She left a legacy of helping others—not just through her work at the foundation but also in how she lived out her life with her motto: because it is the right thing to do.

It was a double hit because it had been eight short weeks since Jeanne had lost her husband, Neal Patterson, Cerner's cofounder and CEO, to soft tissue cancer. The disease had come on fast in the preceding year. Considered curable, he had attacked it with an aggressive treatment plan, but the disease returned. His sudden passing hit the company at its core as Neal was a visionary leader, forging the path to digitize health care—it was truly a founder-led company.

Neal had an uncanny ability to get your attention and inspire when speaking about the health care system and patient experience. He often used Jeanne's health struggles as an example of the need for transformation in this industry. "Health care ultimately becomes personal," he would proclaim. He was filled with passion and optimism that his company would solve the problem.

I once witnessed Neal take the stage, captivating thousands with his unique charisma and charm, as he demonstrated the cumbersome routine he and Jeanne faced at each of her doctors' appointments. They would lug around a heavy briefcase filled with her medical records, highlighting the lack of connectivity within the health care industry that only interoperability could revolutionize. Never did Neal seem defeated. He chose to be optimistic and opportunistic whenever he found a piece of the puzzle to fix health care's deeply rooted challenges. "Health care is too important to stay the same," he would say.

They were part of a familiar and frustrating cycle of patients being responsible for bringing all their information to each visit, every time, as no single physician had access to their complete medical history. Instead, doctors only had fragmented pieces of data to base their decisions on. Incomplete data means incomplete diagnoses and incomplete care.

This hit home: as a child I had seen my mom do this very thing for my dad during his cancer journey. Except she didn't know how to attain the paper records, electronic records, or a CD, so she would take vigorous handwritten notes and carry those to every appointment. She had to use her voice even in the hardest moments. She had to be his advocate.

In the weeks after Jeanne's passing, I worked with my team at the foundation to help support Jeanne's family in the celebration of her life and memorial services. We replicated something we had done for Neal and worked with an organization to manufacture bracelets with their associate numbers (employee ID numbers), initials, and a keyword. Neal's was 001, NLP, and LEGACY. Jeanne's was 007, JML, and LOVE. Her favorite color was pink and her signature flower knockout roses.

That time was an emotional blur. I had worked with the company for 15 years, and they had been our fearless leaders. I couldn't believe they were both gone.

A few weeks following Jeanne's funeral that fall, the foundation hosted its annual Masquerade Ball. The ball benefited the foundation's mission to close the gaps in health care for children around the world. It was a huge fundraising event that both Jeanne and Neal had loved. The Masquerade was an incredible and premier event for the associates (employees), business partners, and community.

That year we pivoted quickly to reimagine the theme. The event was called the 2017 Masquerade Ball: 007. It had the flair of James Bond while honoring our founder with her 007 associate number. It was a beautiful celebration dedicated to her with an additional tribute to Neal. It was meaningful and mission focused.

That evening, as I walked into the Union Station Grand Hall, I felt proud. The team had done their job very well and created a chic, romantic, mysterious, and swoon-worthy event. I looked around the room before the guests arrived and took another sip of my coffee, hoping with every drink that it would prime me with the energy I needed for the night. I was in a daze, which I needed to fix. I had to keep my smile, meet people, thank everyone, and stand on stage to give a 45-minute presentation. I had to be the hostess with the mostest and try my hardest to hit our fundraising goal. Yet, I couldn't shake my fog of exhaustion.

I heard footsteps behind me and turned to see Ashley, an intelligent, beautiful bombshell blonde in the body of a pixie with the height to match. She towers at just over five feet tall and moves at turbo speed when she needs to. She is hands down the best event planner there is, and her peppy and kind personality is the icing on the cake.

She gave me a big hug with a notebook in hand and asked, "Can you believe how beautiful it is?"

"Yes," I said. "Because you did it!"

"We all did it!" she responded like the true sweet human she is.

We chatted for a few minutes about the run of the show, and then she said, "You have to go get dressed! You have 30 minutes before you start greeting all the guests!" I quickly hurried to the designated room to change, taking a few deep breaths on my way to help clear the fog I felt in my head. I slipped on my dress, freshened my makeup, and gave my hair a finishing touch brush. I was ready! My emerald green halter neck gown had been my mother-in-law's. It was sexy, yet classy, timeless, and helped me play the part of a true James Bond girl. I took one last look in the mirror and smiled. I thought, *Even if you are so tired, you look pretty damn good.*

Ashley walked with me to the entrance, and right before they opened the doors, I squeezed her hand and said, "Let's have a great night for the kiddos out there who need our help, and also for our founders. This year is one we won't ever forget."

In true Ashley form she started to cry, and I laughed and said, "Don't, because I am trying really hard not to do just that!." I gave her hand a squeeze and said, "Hey, you know I feel really blessed to do what I do. We sort of have the dream job, Ashley. This event has such a bigger purpose. We help sick kids get to the care that they need—we really are making a difference."

I gave her a big smile and said, "Okay, I will stop with the mush—just thank you for all that you do. This is special."

She teared up again and said, "Well, now my makeup needs to be redone! You are amazing, and I love you. Which I don't think anyone ever says to their manager, but I do! Bring home the contributions on stage tonight, and then let's have a drink." We hugged, and the doors opened.

I stood at the entrance as our guests poured in and greeted each one with a joy-filled smile. My smile was real, but it took every ounce of energy I had. I had to force my brain to smile. I felt disconnected; the fog was looming over me, getting thicker by the minute. But somehow I kept going that night.

The cocktail hour ended, the guests had taken their seats, and it was almost time for the stage presentation to begin. I knew the presentation would be awesome. I loved being on the mic, and I had an incredible team supporting me behind the production booth. I walked up the stage stairs and looked out at the sea of tables with the hundreds of faces of people I knew so well—family, friends, colleagues, community members. It was an incredible feeling to see them all there supporting our foundation's work, specifically this year.

I grabbed the microphone and started to talk, immediately feeling that rush I get from public speaking. I gave a heartfelt welcome, walked the length of the stage as I made a few opening jokes, and laid out how the night would go. So far so good. The audience and I were connected. I went on to thank all the event's top sponsors, our special guests, and our supportive . . . supportive . . . supportive . . .

What is happening?

I forgot a word.

I lost a word.

Why can't I say that word?

My brain knew the word, but I couldn't get it to come out of my mouth. I could not form a single word in that moment. This only lasted a few seconds, but for me it felt like minutes on end. Like those dreams where you're trying to run through heavy mud and can't move your feet? I was stuck in mind mud and had no clue what was happening or how to get out.

What I experienced that night may have been aphasia: the loss of ability to understand or express speech. While it usually happens after a head injury, according to the Mayo Clinic, aphasia can also come on gradually from a slow-growing brain tumor or a disease that causes progressive or permanent damage.

The word I lost in that moment was *community*, "Thank you to our supportive community." It is ironic that I lost the word "community." Over the course of the previous years, every doctor's appointment, misdiagnosis, and symptom I was coping with slowly swallowed my connection to community—my family, colleagues, friends. It was also this community who rallied around me during and after surgery. The fact that this is the first word my brain and my body lost the ability to say now seems fitting.

I got off stage and headed straight to the back room instead of staying out front to talk with major donors and attendees. I was shocked and scared by what had just happened. I sat at a table and focused on breathing. I closed my eyes and repeated my default mantra: *You are fine. Everything is going to be fine.*

About 30 minutes later, I made myself get up from the table. I went to the main ballroom to find my husband and family among the nearly 1500 guests. When I found them, Jeff gave me a glass of white wine, I put on a big smile, and started talking to people.

Mid-conversation, I took a sip of the wine and couldn't swallow it. The wine just sat inside my mouth feeling like acid. I nearly choked and had to turn around and spit it back into my glass. I wiped my mouth with a cocktail napkin and quickly excused myself.

I walked to the closest bathroom, got a cold paper towel, and put it on the back of my neck as a few over-served women walked in. *At least they were having fun.*

I looked in the mirror and felt the loud alarm sounding in my body. I was not crazy, my symptoms were real, this weird night of events was real, and something was not right. I just knew it. I needed help.

I later learned that my tumor was compressing my brain stem and affecting vital functions, including taste and swallowing.

I left that night frightened of my own body and more determined than ever to keep pushing for answers. I couldn't stop, and I knew it. I knew it with my whole being. My body hadn't been trying to scare me. It had been throwing out a final distress signal—Whiskey Tango Foxtrot!

I heard my inner voice loud and clear. I trusted it at that moment even though I was terrified inside what felt like the abyss of the unknown. Now I was determined to make someone listen.

About a week later, I walked into the medical building at the local university hospital to see the professor of otolaryngology (head and neck surgery, or ENT). As I waited in the exam room, I was pleasantly surprised at how nice the office felt. The bright colors of the room and the pictures on the wall had a little more life to it, and it calmed me.

The doctor knocked before entering, and my heart jumped. He came in with a smile and immediately sat down and introduced himself, giving me the opportunity to do the same. He wasn't in a rush, and it seemed he really was interested in knowing who I was. He was looking at me, not his notes or laptop he brought with him, but me. I had his full attention.

Nervous energy coursed through my body as I sat in the doctor's office, fingers fiddling anxiously with my wedding ring as both hands rested on a notebook I had brought. The notebook didn't have all my medical documents, but it had my notes. My timeline. It was my story that I decided to write down.

He asked me to recount my symptoms and what led to this appointment. With a deep breath, I began to speak.

"It's been a long journey," I started, "with countless appointments and multiple issues that just don't seem right. My issues seem to always center around my ear and head, but we haven't found any answers." My voice wavered slightly as I tried to downplay the severity of the situation, knowing deep down that I was not being honest with myself or the doctor. Yet, I couldn't bring myself to fully express the fear and uncertainty that consumed me.

I continued, "Sometimes I feel healthy-ish, but other times something just feels off." As soon as the words left my lips, I regretted them. How could I expect to find answers if I couldn't even advocate for myself properly? I fully recognized in that moment that I was giving in to the fear of rejection, disappointment, and dismissal. It is terrifying to be the patient and have to recount everything to yet another doctor—*No one before had listened, so why would this one be different?*

No. No, Shanna, No! I heard that voice—my voice—deep down say.

I hesitated for maybe a count of three.

I took a sharp deep breath and found the courage to speak my truth. I opened the notebook on my lap where I had documented information from my appointments, symptoms, and pain points along the way. The notes were scattered, but I knew them by heart. I looked at them for just a glance and said, "Actually, no. No, things don't just feel off. In fact, I don't believe I am healthy at all. Something is seriously wrong, and it has been for a very long time, and it is getting worse."

The weight of those words hung heavy in the air as I awaited the doctor's response, heart racing with both fear and a glimmer of hope.

He simply leaned in and said, "Tell me more."

I told the doctor everything; what happened at the Masquerade, my episodes of severe vertigo, the dizzy spells, walking with a slant, flashes of light, sickness, and the hearing loss. I even told him that I was exhausted from searching for an answer and feeling dismissed. I told him that I almost felt hopeless and what drove me to seek out his help was the interview with Savannah and Maria from *The Today Show*.

I finished by saying, "Something has been off for so long. You probably think I am crazy, but I feel like I have all the symptoms of a brain tumor."

"I don't think you're crazy. It's never crazy to look for answers. That is your right as a patient, and it is my job as a provider to listen and find them," he said with conviction and a genuine smile. I could have jumped out of my chair and given him the biggest hug. I wanted an answer, but, before that, I wanted someone to confirm that it was my right to search for that answer.

He stood up and walked over to me, holding a device up to my right ear to look inside. As he did this he said, "Tell me again what this ear feels like."

"It feels full, like constant pressure. Sometimes it's better, sometimes it's worse, but it is always there. If I try to use my phone on that side, it's not just hearing loss I notice, but people sound underwater."

"Interesting," he responded. "By just looking at it, your ear looks fine, but that doesn't mean it is."

I felt safe with this doctor. He was really listening to me, empathizing with my struggle and pain, and not ruling anything out just yet.

He lightly touched the right side of my face and asked if I had any numbness or asleep sensations.

"No. Not at all."

He smiled and replied, "Well, that is good."

Was it good? I seemed to be passing all the tests. Again.

"Let's have you stand up and stand over at this far corner of the room. I want you to close your eyes, put your arms straight out in front of you, and march in place for a slow count of 10 seconds."

I gave him a little laugh and said, "Okay, that seems easy enough."

Admittedly, I felt a little funny as I marched in place for about 10 seconds, wondering what the purpose of this exercise was. I opened my eyes before he got to 10, because I hit something. The wall.

He looked at the attending resident who had come into the room a few minutes earlier and then at me and said, "Did you know that you moved to the other side of the room?"

I hadn't at all. I was shocked. *How did I move this far and not know it?* I thought. I looked around to get my bearings. I had walked toward the left side of the room as if my body was pulling me that way and hit the wall.

The doctor said we should do an MRI. He placed his hand gently behind my right ear and said, "I think it is possible we could find something very small right back here sitting on your hearing nerve." I wasn't exactly sure what he meant, but he explained it calmly, so I was calm.

Instead of having the order passed off to a nurse to call and someone from the exam center calling me later that week, he scheduled it right there himself. It was Friday morning, and he said he would like me to do it during an opening at the end of the day that following Monday.

I left the office and for the first time felt validated in the years of feelings and symptoms, wondering whether this would point me to an answer. Someone had listened to me and did not take inconclusive as an answer. I wasn't crazy.

I also had that feeling—that feeling when you are in complete darkness, but you know that someone or something is right in front of you or maybe behind you. I wondered what would come next.

November 2017: Lost in the Impossible

I hate this machine. Hate it. That was all I could think as they inserted me into the small rotating tube with a guard over my face and earphones on my head.

My anxiety was through the roof, and it pulsed through my veins like a high voltage wire. It didn't help that it was an unforgiving wintry Monday morning in November, the kind that makes you want to crawl back into bed and never leave. The bitter cold air bit at my skin, and to my dismay, I learned that the MRI machine was in an attached trailer outside the main building.

My heart raced as I stepped outside, hastily wrapping my coat around my shivering frame. This was not the patient experience I had hoped for. My anxiety only intensified at the thought of being enclosed in the dreaded machine, my body still and restricted while loud, clanging noises echoed around me.

I knew I had to do this, for my health and for my peace of mind. So I braced myself and trudged toward the trailer, trying to ignore the biting cold and the anxious thoughts swirling in my head. As I entered the trailer, I took a deep breath to calm my nerves.

The room was tiny, I was freezing, and I wanted to run. But I had to be there. I just needed to get it over with. Maybe I was crazy, but I knew something was not right. I also knew that every doctor and specialist I had seen over the course of six years thought nothing was wrong. I felt *wrong*. I was told I had allergies, sinus infections, even that I was just a tired and overworked mom. I knew it had to be something more.

It felt that my body was sounding an alarm that only I could hear. If it weren't for the interview I had seen on *The Today Show*, I wouldn't have been at this appointment about to be inserted into the most intimidating machine the modern medical world has to offer for brain scans. Here I was, and I needed to know if there was something the doctors had been missing.

I was shaking and trying not to move anything. If I did, I was told they would have to start over again. I had to lie perfectly still. No sudden movements and no talking. The face guard that had just been clicked into place solidified my emotions of being a patient without a voice for years, and now all I wanted to do was fucking scream.

As I lay on the cold, hard surface of the MRI machine, unable to find a comfortable position, I yearned for some sense of comfort. Fortunately, the technician by my side was a ray of light in this otherwise dreary situation. In these small moments, caregivers truly are heroes. Despite the terrifying contraption looming over me, she exuded warmth and empathy through her gentle touch and kind words. Her Russian accent was soft and calming. As she spoke to me through the microphone, I couldn't help but think of the scene from *Armageddon* where Lev, a Russian character played by Peter Stormare, gets frustrated and yells out, "This is how we fix things in a Russian space station!" The thought made me smile and almost laugh—momentarily distracting me from my nerves. Almost.

She told me the test was going to take 45 minutes—one test without the contrast fluid and one test with—and, for what felt like the hundredth time, that if I moved, they were going to have to repeat it. I would have to lie there and only shake internally for 45 minutes, all the while feeling as if I were in a coffin.

This was my first MRI, and my second brain scan if you count the CT scan I'd had less than a year ago at a local hospital. There was nothing unusual discovered in the CT, so that gave me the tiniest sliver of comfort in this moment.

The machine turned on and sounded like a lawn mower in my head. I squeezed my eyes shut tight. I prayed and clenched my teeth. The one positive was that it wasn't loud in my right ear since I had started to lose some hearing. I had been told my hearing loss could be from a series of different things—from chronic ear infections and Ménière's disease to damage caused by the intense decibel level I endured as a Kansas City Chiefs cheerleader for eight seasons.

I could deal with all those potential issues. I just hoped that this brain scan wouldn't show something else.

"Shanna," the technician's voice came through the machine speaker. "You are doing excellent. The first half without the contrast is done. Now you will feel warm from the contrast, and we will start the second half of the process."

She was right, I did feel warm and sort of like I peed my pants, adding to my discomfort.

My breathing slowed down as the end of the MRI neared. I told myself to breathe and tried to concentrate on the groceries I had to get after this awful moment, making a mental list in my head: rotisserie chicken, baking potatoes, broccoli . . . chocolate. Lots of chocolate.

The MRI ended, and the technician helped me out of the machine. As mentioned, the exam trailer was small. Really small. The door to the room where she was reviewing the images was open, and I saw the image of my brain, which included a large blur. *That didn't seem right.*

I felt it again. The feeling that something was off, and only I knew it. A rare but familiar moment of mind and body alignment. I shook off the feeling, got dressed, and left.

I tried to call my husband, Jeff, but he was still at work and didn't answer. I needed to talk to someone and get some affirmation that all was going to be fine. I knew in my core something was wrong, but I didn't want to believe something could be wrong with my brain. *This was just another test that had to be done*, I assured myself. But I wanted someone else to tell me that.

At that moment, one of my best buddies, Josh, called. He started off with a lame joke, as usual. I fake laughed and told him what I just did.

"Dude," he said in his lifelong surfer accent that belied his Missouri roots. "Dude, you are fine. It is over, and it will be fine."

He was right, it would be fine.

It would be fine.

It. Would. Be. Fine.

I skipped the store that day and decided it would be a leftover night. I was too tired to cook.

As I walked into my house 25 minutes after leaving the exam, I put my purse on the counter and my cell phone rang. It was the ENT specialist from the university hospital who had ordered the MRI. I thought it was odd he was calling so quickly but figured he just wanted to tell me that the scan had turned out, like Josh said, fine. That would be great!

I answered with a smile, and in just a few short seconds after a pleasant greeting, he said, "Shanna, there is something there, and it is big. We need you back in the office tomorrow to discuss the diagnosis and care plan."

As if time stopped, my entire world condensed into a single point. Like being trapped in a dark box with no escape, my senses were overwhelmed and my vision tunneled. The acrid taste of fear coated my tongue, making it feel thick and heavy. My heart raced inside my chest, each beat louder and more frantic than the last. It reverberated through every inch of my body, drowning out any other sounds around me. I desperately tried to speak but only managed a strained gasp as panic constricted my throat. Everything else faded away as I struggled to catch my breath and make sense of what was happening.

The doctor's voice broke through the overwhelming noise in my head, his words barely registering through the haze of terror. "Shanna, are you there? Did you hear me?"

It was as if I was being pulled into the center of a storm, my body struggling against the invisible force pressing in on me. I clung to the counter as if it were the only solid thing in a world that was spinning out of control. My eyes closed; I focused all my energy on the simple act of breathing, trying to steady myself enough to understand the words being spoken to me.

I listened to him while every breath felt harder to take in, as if someone had punched me in the gut. It was a rare brain tumor, he confirmed, and they were hopeful it was benign. Usually, these kinds of tumors were manageable because they are slow growing.

However, mine had outgrown the opportunity to be managed and was now considered giant for a tumor of this kind. It had most likely been growing on my hearing nerve for 5–10 years. It was golf-ball sized, roughly 4.5 cm, and compressing my brainstem.

My throat constricted, gasping for air as I heard his words. My body frozen in shock, unable to move or escape from this nightmare. Rage boiled within me, consuming every inch of my being until I felt as if I might explode. For years, I had searched for answers and been dismissed, while an imposter grew inside my head, stealing my life away one day at a time. The tears streamed relentlessly down my cheeks, from sorrow, pain, and fury, and I felt myself on the brink of a primal scream.

I had a brain tumor. A brain tumor. A large and rare brain tumor. It had been one minute since I walked through my front door thinking about leftovers.

That was *before*.

This was the incomprehensible and terrifying *after*.

My future vanished into the darkness—hope seemed hard to grasp, and I was paralyzed with fear just as I had been in front of that bear.

It all seemed impossible.

Audacious Optimism in Action

The journey that truly developed my understanding of audacious optimism began with the gut-wrenching news of my brain tumor diagnosis. The thread of positivity, woven throughout my entire life, was on the verge of snapping as I struggled to accept this turning point. Years of searching for answers almost seemed futile at that moment. But it also revealed the true power of choice and forced me to dig deep and listen to my inner voice, while embracing the daunting unknown. Faced with a loss of control, I fought to find a way forward, determined to reclaim my agency and boldly declare my intentions and vision for my future. It was a defining moment where I had to summon every ounce of strength.

At some point in your life you may have faced challenges and obstacles where you felt stripped of the ability to move forward and choose optimism—whether on a health journey or in the face of other major life changes. There is still hope, and you always have the ability to reach for it.

Tips on how to choose audacious optimism and navigate life's journey:

- **Believe yourself:** Trust the stirring in your soul and the fluttering in your gut, even if they go against the logical reasoning of others. Don't brush them off as irrational; instead, take a moment to reflect and ask yourself, "What is my intuition truly telling me?" Believe yourself and trust that inner voice that speaks to you, for it is rooted in your subconscious knowledge, deepest desires, and core values.

- **Accept and excel:** Emotions are an inherent part of the human experience. From sadness to anger, we can feel a range of intense feelings. Before deciding to approach situations with optimism, it is necessary to first acknowledge and accept your emotions. Imagine you're feeling overwhelmed at work due to tight deadlines and high expectations. Take a moment to acknowledge your stress. Understand that it's a natural response to pressure. Instead of berating yourself, say, "It's okay to feel stressed. I'm human." Use this self-awareness to strategize. Break down tasks, prioritize, and focus on one thing at a time. Take the time to find inner harmony before moving forward. This act of self-compassion is crucial in order to not only accept but also excel!

- **Persist with patience:** When faced with challenges, audacious optimism requires both persistence and patience. Keep pressing onward, even when you don't see instant results, and be willing to grow slow. Start by identifying your ultimate goal. Whether it's a personal project, career advancement, or health related, be specific about what you want to achieve. Divide your goal into smaller, manageable tasks. These are small steps toward your larger goal. For example, if your goal is to write a book, break it down into chapters or sections. If you're working on physical health, break it down into daily workouts or weekly milestones. Assign deadlines to each smaller task. These deadlines should be challenging yet achievable. Remember that progress takes time, so be patient with yourself. Patience does not equal apathy; it means staying dedicated even while taking the time for change to occur.

- **Stare down the bear:** In life, there will be times when you come face-to-face with something as intimidating and daunting as a bear in the thick of the woods. Your instinctual responses kick in: fight, flight, or freeze. It could be as simple as waking up to confront a difficult day or as significant as a major life event. But just like with a real bear, running away won't solve anything; you must stand your ground and face it head-on. Remind yourself that you are capable and strong enough to overcome this challenge. In moments of doubt, look at yourself in the mirror and reaffirm your determination to succeed, saying, "I will make it through this day" or "I will overcome this sadness." Don't allow yourself to give up or take the easy way out by stuffing it down and pivoting away. Instead, muster the courage to stare down this bear until it moves out of your way.

- **Use your voice and claim your space:** Speak your truth boldly and stand tall in your own space. Confidence is built through the brave act of expression and owning your rightful place. Let your voice ring out, loud and proud, for both you and those around you to hear. Every day, maybe in the mornings, before you start your Zoom calls, or before you get in your car, embrace your presence; literally stretch out your arms, stand taller, hold your head up and expand beyond what you feel capable of, and fill the room with your bold, confident energy.

Audacious optimism may not come easily, but it's worth pursuing. Choosing this bold and courageous mindset is not taking the easy way out; it's taking action to pave the path for growth and progress toward a brighter future.

Trust Yourself

Your inner voice, also known as intuition or gut feeling, is a source of wisdom and true feelings that originates from within. It serves as a personal guide to help you navigate life's challenges and opportunities, and many times serves as an inner alarm. By trusting yourself, you are placing faith in your own ability to make good decisions and (maybe even subconsciously) anticipating positive results, which is a reflection of an optimistic mindset.

In this fast-paced world, it can be easy to lose touch with our inner voice. The hustle and bustle of daily life often drowns out the soft whispers of our intuition, leaving us feeling lost and unsure of ourselves. By learning to trust and listen to our inner voice, we can tap into the tools of strength and courage that allow us to take charge of our lives.

We all know someone who always relies on others for decision-making or struggles to speak up for themselves. These individuals lack trust in their own intuition and are often at the mercy of external forces. I have personally found myself in this position countless times!

Our inner voice is like a constant companion, guiding our thoughts and actions as we navigate through life's ups and downs. When we choose optimism and believe in ourselves, our inner dialogue becomes positive and motivating, propelling us toward success. However, when negative self-talk takes over, it can diminish our confidence and hinder our ability to trust our intuition and make good decisions.[1]

By learning to trust in our inner voice, we build resilience and become more comfortable confronting the unknown and facing challenges head-on. Being true to ourselves, even in the face of potential failure, gives us a sense of accomplishment and reinforces our optimistic mindset. This, in turn, encourages us to continue trusting our intuition and embracing all that life has to offer.

Here are a few ways to cultivate trust in your inner voice:

Challenge negative thoughts: When you catch yourself thinking negatively, question the validity of that thought. What has made you start thinking that way? What event, comment or challenge trigged those thoughts? Can you replace it with a more positive perspective?

Reflect on good decisions: Take a moment to remember times when your intuition has led you in the right direction. Acknowledge and celebrate those successes as proof that your inner voice is reliable.

Listen to your body: Pay attention to how your body feels, such as tension or relaxation, when making decisions. These are helpful and valid cues from your inner voice—your alarm!

Seek external validation sparingly: While external opinions can be valuable, don't rely solely on it. What do YOU want? What do YOU need? What do YOU feel? It's important to listen to your own inner wisdom, and this includes limiting the value you put in social media engagement.

Trusting your inner voice is a testament to your belief in the potential for great things to happen in your life and your capability to create them. It is a fundamental element of optimism—for choosing optimism is, in fact, putting trust in yourself and your future. Throughout my life, I have repeatedly learned the importance of trusting myself. When I relied too heavily on outside opinions or prioritized the approval of others over my own inner voice, I inevitably faced setbacks, frustration, and disappointment.

Now, looking back on my journey, there were pivotal moments, which started in my childhood, where listening to my own instincts led me toward the path that was meant for me.

Note

1. https://experteditor.com.au/blog/the-psychology-of-the-inner-voice-9-insights-into-how-it-shapes-our-decisions

My Roots

I looked out my window and what did I see?
Popcorn popping on an apricot tree.
It wasn't really so, but it seemed to be.
Popcorn popping on an apricot tree.

—*Georgia Bello*

I was raised as a member of the Church of Jesus Christ of Latter-day Saints (LDS) in Liberty, Missouri. My hometown started as a small rural community in the Midwest along the loosely defined path of Tornado Alley. We were surrounded by fields, and hundreds of trees that rolled with the gentle hills of the Missouri River Valley onward to the Rockies. In spring, all the scattered trees burst into bloom making them look like fields of giant green popcorn balls. This always reminded me of the uplifting song that all LDS children learned to sing about how faith can make beautiful miracles happen like popcorn popping on the apricot trees.

My mom would make sure we always had our "tornado clothes" ready, just in case the sirens began to blare and we had to head down to the dank, spidery basement, to huddle together around a portable TV and wait out the storm. We lived in a perpetual state of disaster preparedness, always peripherally aware of the possibility for catastrophe, and yet, when it finally did strike, it took us all by surprise.

When I was young, Liberty was still a small town with tiny suburban enclaves nestled between wheat fields, cows pastures, and small family-owned businesses. There was a four-way cross where you could see a few local banks, Crowley Furniture, a couple of truck stops, Bob's IGA, and Gary Crossley Ford, where I worked detailing cars when I was 18.

At the center of town is the historic Liberty square, where the farmers market and festivals were held. People gathered there in October for the Fall Festival and in April for Spring on the Square. There were parades for everything, and once I started taking dance classes, I would march with my troupe in every single one, throwing out candy to the cheering crowds along North Main Street. I even marched in the fake parade staged for Stephen King's thriller movie set in a Midwest farm town called *Sometimes They Come Back*.

I grew up on the corner of Melrose Lane in the neighborhood of Wilshire, and it was my whole world until it wasn't. Our house was cute and well kept thanks to my dad. I remember Fourth of July there with my whole family coming over to shoot off fireworks; my grandma making ice cream in the churn, my mom and aunts cooking, and my dad and uncles playing with us in the pool. I would ride around the neighborhood with one of my Wilshire friends—leaving our bikes everywhere and anywhere and going down to the neighborhood park only to jump in the creek and collect crawdads. It had all the charms of a small town as well as a strict social class division and a well-greased gossip mill. Even with a population boom in the early 2000s, Liberty will always be frozen in time for me. It'll always be how I remember it in my childhood as long as tornadoes keep missing it.

Liberty holds a special significance for members of the LDS church because the prophet Joseph Smith sat in the Liberty Jail over the long cold winter of 1838–1839. That spring though, by the time the trees had bloomed, Joseph Smith and the church leaders were allowed to escape for political reasons. This escape followed the instatement of the Missouri Executive Order 44 (known as the Mormon extermination order—rescinded in 1976 for being unconstitutional by Missouri Governor Kit Bond). Smith and the church followers fled to Nauvoo, Illinois, where they stayed for seven years before Smith was martyred and church followers left to settle in Salt Lake City, Utah.

I loved going to church with my family. It felt like we were part of a community. I felt safe and supported. I remember sitting through long church services, along with the dozens of kids in the congregation. There were numerous kids in every family. It was amazing to me. When I think back to those Sundays, I remember the smell of Cheerios that my mom and many moms brought in Ziploc bags to keep all the kids busy, and the smell of sweet, toasted oats filled the church.

The inside of the sanctuary felt heavenly to me at that age. It had three columns of rows and an altar with a piano, and a hymnal board beside the pianist's head to tell us what hymns we were going to sing that Sunday. There was never just one person who spoke on Sundays. I remember them having certain leaders speaking, and then some Sundays anyone could speak if they felt called by the Lord to testify. Many times, these testimonials would result in grown-ups crying right in front of the whole congregation, which made many of us kids feel wiggly and uncomfortable, but sometimes I felt intrigued to know more about them. They always ended with an expression of faith, deep and tested.

"I know this church is true," everyone would say in conclusion. And I would think with my curious child mind, "Really? How can you be so sure?"

My favorite part of the service was when it was time for sacrament because after they blessed the bread and water, they would pass it around in these cute little trays. I would take a crumb of bread and then pick up the tiniest little cup of water and drink it. You were supposed to throw it back in the tray, but sometimes I would ask my mom whether I could keep the cup to play with, and she would answer me with a wink, as I slid the cup into my pocket.

I loved spending the night at my cousin's house and then going to the afternoon service with them. They had a family of nine, and that felt huge compared to my family of five. They would all crowd into one row. I loved all my cousins, and it was thrilling to be able to sit with them. I would always sit right next to my cousin Amanda, who is nine months younger than me. She was bossy and beautiful, and she was my best friend. I loved her like a sister, even though we were opposites. Where I was always positive and peppy, Amanda was cool, which meant she was moody and ornery.

Amanda was beautiful with the shiniest brown hair. I was still stuck in my awkward childhood years. I would smile up to my eyes whenever I caught sight of her. I don't know if she got as excited to see me. With Amanda, it was always hard to tell. Regardless, I would smile big enough for the both of us.

When I was eight years old, it was my turn to be baptized. Most LDS children are baptized at age eight because that is thought to be the "age of accountability," or when a child knows the difference between right and wrong. This was a big moment in the church, and in every LDS child's life.

For my baptism, my Uncle Jim performed the ordinance, and my dad assisted. My uncle had me put one hand on his arm, and my dad held my other hand.

"Sister Shanna Michelle Hilt," my uncle Jim said, pronouncing every one of my names carefully, like he wanted God to be sure to remember me—thank you, Uncle Jim. "Having been commissioned by Jesus Christ, I baptize you in the name of the Father, the Son, and the Holy Ghost."

Then my dad covered my nose with both our hands and held my head. He dipped me carefully backward into the water until my entire body was submerged. Then he quickly lifted me up. Everyone cheered as I came up out of the water. I looked at my dad and my uncle and smiled with tears in my eyes—the newest member of the community. It was incredibly special.

After the baptism, I changed into dry clothing and went back into the room. Then, in front of all the attendees, I was blessed with the gift of the Holy Ghost. I sat in a chair, and my uncle and dad placed their hands on my head. Then my uncle gave me the blessing of the Holy Ghost, who would be with me for the rest of my life.

Afterward, we had a reception where my parents gifted me a white Bible with my name engraved in gold. It was a touching moment that I will always treasure, along with the Bible itself. My parents were beaming with pride, and it made me happy to see them happy. Yet, amid all these emotions, my youthful mind was racing. *What comes next? Will everything suddenly make sense? Are there certain expectations of me now?* My little heart and mind wrestled with unidentified pressures and anticipations of this declaration of faith.

However, my search for faith did not begin with my baptism. The decision to leave the LDS church and its teachings came later, but the seeds of curiosity and inquisitiveness had been planted within me already at a young age. It started many years earlier—possibly when I first learned of my father's illness. There is a profound impact on a child experiencing their first heartache or fear related to a loved one; although it is painful, it can also lead to an awakening of emotions.

The day is etched in my memory as if it were yesterday. I was just six years old, fresh from a half-day of kindergarten and eager to return home. My mom wasn't home yet, but my dad was there, a rare treat as his job kept him traveling three days out of every week. He worked as a customer service agent for the airlines in St. Louis, a job he loved and worked tirelessly at. His early arrival home that day was a thrill for me. As I burst through the door, I ran into his waiting arms and exclaimed, "Daddy!" As he gazed down at me with his usual warm smile, I noticed a flicker of confusion in his eyes.

Despite recognizing me as his daughter, he struggled to recall my name. Fear exploded in my heart as I realized something was very wrong. Drawing on the emergency drills my mom had taught me, I called 911 without hesitating and kept a level head. The ambulance arrived just as my mother returned home. As they got my dad in the ambulance, my mom pulled me into a hug and said, "I'm so proud of you, Honey. Great job trusting your instincts." After I am sure I looked at her questioning what the word "instincts" meant, she said with a weary smile as she pointed at my heart, "That little voice that lives inside of you that you trusted when it said take action."

Although it turned out to be a complication related to an old head injury from playing football years earlier, this episode served as a warning sign to the doctors that there may be more going on with my dad's health.

A few short months later, my dad was diagnosed with cancer—leukemia. They never sat us kids down and told us that my dad was ill. My mom always said, "Your dad just had another doctor's appointment, but he's fine." He wasn't fine, but I don't think any of us knew how to comprehend or explain this. Not even my parents. My brothers and I had to go to family therapy, where we would talk about things and how we felt about my dad being sick. Our parents always seemed to talk over us in these sessions. They didn't want to scare us with too much information.

I know I had no idea what was really happening with my dad. My older brothers, Erik and Steven, understood. But I never caught on that my dad was going to die. Steven remembers the therapist asking my parents, "Do they know yet that Gene will . . . ?"

"No," my dad chimed in. "We don't think they know."

Steven said at that moment he looked at me, with a peppy smile on my face, and he could see that I had no clue what was coming.

My childhood bedroom was tiny and pink. I could walk across it in about 15 steps. It was only big enough for a twin bed, but it was cozy, and I loved it. Around my birthday, just seven days after my dad's, and right before Christmas in 1988, my parents told me that Daddy needed to sleep in my room from now on. They moved his brown La-Z-Boy recliner into my room and set it right beside my bed. He had his gray metal oxygen tanks beside his recliner and a couple of small waste baskets that were constantly full of wadded up Kleenex. My dad was always coughing up something. On most nights, I would inevitably doze off on the living room couch while watching a movie. With a gentle hand, my mom would wake me and guide me to her room, where I would find peace in the comfort of her presence. My dad's appearance, smell, and behavior had started to frighten and confuse me, making my mom's bed seem like the only haven in the world. It was my sanctuary from the chaos.

We had a small suburban home with five people and one bathroom. You could hear everything from anywhere in the house. I would lie awake and listen to my dad coughing and say silent prayers asking God to make my dad better. My dad was so sick that it was hard to do much as a family or even go to church, yet somehow, he was still traveling to work. He kept that up until six weeks before he died. He loved his job, he loved interacting with people, helping them to get to where they were going. My dad loved being useful, he loved people, and he loved life.

My dad's supervisor called my mom in early March of 1989 because I think he feared my dad would drop dead at his post. "Reina, I need your help," he said a little uncomfortably, I'm sure. "We love Gene, but he is so sick. We even got him a stool so he can sit down throughout the day while he helps customers, but even that seems to be too hard for him. I think we need him to retire."

My mom knew that my dad would be heartbroken—that he would see retiring as giving up on life. But she talked my dad into it, and the airline gave him a retirement party. The first week he was home, instead of sitting in the chair all day as he had done on his days off, he told my mom, "Well, Reina, I'm home, and I am determined to be of use."

That energetic promise was inspiring and didn't last long. My dad became extraordinarily frail and weak within just a few days. Here was a guy who had been an athlete, an entrepreneur, and an adventurer who had worked hard his whole life. The cancer turned him to skin and bones and aged him 30 years in just a couple of months. I remember one day in early April I walked past my room and saw my dad in his chair. He was skinny, wearing a worn Kansas City Chiefs shirt partially exposed under his usual comfy long dark blue robe. He had both arms on the arms of the chair and his head lowered in defeat.

NO! I thought to myself. I was not going to let my dad feel like that. I walked in with a determined smile and sat on my bed across from him. "Daddy. Do you know how to tell if an elephant has been in your fridge?" I asked him, like I was asking him a serious question. A good joke is all about the set up.

"No, I don't," he answered smiling, starting to chuckle, "but I hope you will tell me."

"There are footprints in the peanut butter," I said with a huge smile. And then I started to do this loud and overly exaggerated giggle. It was a terrible performance, but it made my dad laugh out loud. "Sweetie," he said to me and held my hand, "you are an absolute light in this world." I felt so happy that I had found a way to make my daddy happy in one of his saddest moments. If I had taken away his pain for even one minute that was enough for me.

A few weeks later, I now know, my dad got shingles, and he and my mom made the hard decision to admit him to the VA hospital in Kansas City. My mom said they looked at each other, and both knew that he wouldn't be coming home again. She said that every day in the hospital he lost a little bit of life. She went to see my dad that last morning, and he told her how much he loved her and asked her to tell us kids how much he loved us. Then he looked forward at someone who wasn't there and smiled and said, "Okay, I am ready to go." He closed his eyes with a smile still on his face and went.

The sun had barely begun to peek through the curtains covering the bedroom window when I woke up that Sunday, the familiar scent of my mom's room in the air—a combination of eucalyptus and Halls cough drops. But she wasn't there next to me. My oldest brother came into the room with a solemn look on his face. "Mom went to the hospital again," he said. I buried my head back into my pillow and tried to distract myself by reading a book. Suddenly, the doorbell rang, and with pep in my step I made my way downstairs to answer it. To my surprise, it was my aunt Dottie standing on our doorstep. "Hi Aunt Dottie!" I greeted her with enthusiasm. "Are you here to take me to church since mom isn't here?"

Her expression turned somber as she placed a comforting hand on my shoulder. "No, sweetie," she said softly. "Your dad passed away this morning." My heart dropped as tears welled up in my eyes. My mom had asked Aunt Dottie to come take care of us until she could make it home from the hospital. It was then that reality set in, and everything changed in an instant.

My dad died.
What? What did that mean?
Like, he was gone?
Forever?
They said he was fine.

My face must have said it all because my aunt reached for me and pulled me close while ushering me to the couch.

She enveloped me like a warm, comforting blanket. Amid my grief, her strong arms provided a sense of security and solace. My body trembled with sobs, tears streaming down my cheeks and my chest heaving with each breath. "He loved you," she whispered, her voice filled with love and understanding. We sat on the plush couch in front of the sheer blue curtains that filtered in the soft light, creating a dreamy atmosphere. I cried until I had no tears left.

The weight of sudden grief pressed down on me. It broke apart the only world I had known with my loving family, threatening to consume my entire being. Amid these overwhelming emotions and heartache, I felt a faint prompting or nudge in my mind. Like a small voice telling me to move, to put one foot in front of the other. I felt desperate to be somewhere else, a need for movement in a world turned upside down. I looked up at my aunt and with tears streaming down my face choked out the words, "Will you take me to church with your family?" I needed to do something, to be somewhere other than here in this cloud of sadness and grief. She took me while my brothers opted to stay behind.

The kids were all sitting in the Sunday school, and the teacher asked me my name and what brought me to their ward. "My dad died, and I didn't know what else to do today," I told her as I made perfect eye contact. "I just wanted to be here." The teacher looked stunned, and my cousin Amanda grabbed my hand. "You know what?" the teacher gently said. "Let's cancel the lesson and go for a walk. It's a beautiful spring day."

We all walked outside, and the teacher asked me about my dad. I told her that he was a wonderful dad, and that he had a great smile and that I loved him. I told her he had worked for the airlines, both Braniff and then Northwest. That's where he met my mom because she had been a flight attendant while he was on baggage transport and general maintenance. "Why did you want to be here with us today, Shanna?" she asked me.

"Because I'm sad," I said. "My brothers are sad and still sleeping, my mom is at the hospital and has been so sad for a long time. My daddy had been sad, and it made me sad to look at him."

Now sobbing and choking on my words I said, "I don't . . . I don't want to be sad anymore. I want to be happy. When will I be happy?"

She stopped walking and looked at me, holding both my hands. "I'll bet your dad is smiling down on you from Heaven right now, and he also wants his family . . . you, his little girl, to be happy and live your life."

She took a deep breath and said, "I know this may not make sense now, but maybe someday it will. You won't always feel happy, but you can make choices that will lead you to really happy moments. You had a great life with your daddy, and you will always have those incredible memories, and now you will have a great life beyond this moment of pain. Trust me. Actually, trust yourself, because it is telling you that you want to move beyond the sadness, and I believe you will."

I smiled as a choked laugh came out of my mouth through the bitter tears and sobbing. I can't remember that teacher's name, but what she said and did for me in that moment was she gave me permission to accept what had happened and not live in sadness—to make a choice and trust myself to move beyond the pain.

I sang "Families Will Be Together Forever," by Vanja Watkins, with my cousins at my dad's funeral. My mom let me wear a white and pink polka dot dress. She said black was too depressing and she was determined to put us in something bright to celebrate his life. I thought my mom was pretty cool for letting me go with the Easter colors, but the bright tones didn't manage to hold off the dark depression that came next in my house.

I remember watching TV early in the mornings by myself—watching my mom go through the motions of trying to work, sleeping, ordering silver and gold off QVC, then sleeping some more. My diet that year was an unhealthy rotation of spaghetti, potato soup, and Happy Meals. We stopped going to church because my mom needed to rest—she slept a lot. This left me to my own devices, free to design my own activities and schedule.

I would go out to Amanda's house a lot. I'd play all day long but when night came, I would sit and think about all the terrible things that might happen to my mom or my brothers while I wasn't there. And then, like clockwork, I would go into my aunt and uncle's room with overflowing tears and ask them to drive me 30 minutes home at one in the morning. To their credit, they did every single time, except for the last time.

I'd had fun all day running on their land and playing with my cousins, and then night fell. Of course, I walked into my uncle's room like usual, only this time my uncle didn't go looking for his car keys so he could drive me back. Instead, he sat down on the side of the bed by me and gave me a side hug. "Shanna, I will take you home, but first I want to give you a choice," he told me. "Your mom is fine, your brothers are fine, and you may not feel fine, but you are safe. Could you try and sleep for one more hour? Then, if you are still awake, you can come back in here and get me, and I will take you home if that's what you want to do."

Ugg, there was that word again, "fine." I looked at him through my tear-filled eyes, took a deep breath, and said, "Okay, I will." He gave me a big smile and a hug and said, "I know you will."

I was devastated, but I went back to Amanda's room, pulled the covers completely over my head, closed my eyes, and tried one more time to fall asleep. Amazingly, I did. I woke up the next morning to Uncle Jim with a huge smile on his face. "Well, look at that brave girl. I am so happy to see you this morning," he said in his booming, deep voice, and I could see how proud he was of me. I knew that I had broken through something—I wasn't fine, and my feelings and fear had been real, but I had challenged them just by making a choice to try one more time to go back to bed and believe in myself. I also felt proud and I knew that particular fear would not have that much power over me again because I found my courage.

As I matured, my desire to attend church never faded. In fact, it only grew stronger as I began exploring different faiths with my friends. I ventured into Catholic, Baptist, Pentecostal, Presbyterian, and Methodist churches, attended Jewish services, and explored other practices. Each new experience expanded my understanding of the world and its diverse beliefs.

Through these experiences, I realized that each faith had something unique to offer, and at their core they all shared similar values such as love, compassion, forgiveness, service toward others, and a deep connection to hope. It didn't matter what label or denomination a person belonged to—what mattered most was their sincere devotion to perfecting love, doing no harm, and living out these values in their daily lives. Each person's spiritual journey is unique, valid, and it's their own.

While the LDS church still held a special place in my heart, it no longer aligned with what I believed. For years, I had felt defined by the label "Mormon," but now I understood that my faith was personal and independent from any denomination. It was a revelation that left me feeling both liberated and anxious. Would confessing my true beliefs cost me my family's acceptance?

In my very early 20s, over lunch, I mustered up the courage to finally tell my uncle Jim about my changing beliefs. It was a pivotal moment in my journey toward discovering and owning my own faith.

When my dad passed, my Uncle Jim really became the leading voice for our family in the church and in our home. My mom needed support, and she got that emotionally and financially from my aunt and uncle. We had a lot of help from my grandma Dorothy, and my uncle Chuck and aunt Lois were there whenever we needed them. My uncle Jim was a leader in the church, and he was the one person that I always felt accountable to growing up. This was never an accountability he set in motion—it was my own view and respect for him as a beloved figure in my life. I felt that I owed it to him to tell him where I stood. I knew that he was kind, caring, and stern, and I knew he would listen carefully to what I had to say. I was nervous. I worried I would be seen as a disappointment to him and my family.

As I sat across from my uncle Jim at the table, I knew it was now or never. My hands trembled, and as I looked over at him and smiled, I felt like the same scared little girl who years before wanted him to drive her home in the middle of the night. I took a deep breath and told him the truth about my beliefs and belonging to the church.

He took a bite of his sandwich and looked at me with kind eyes. "Okay by me," he said without hesitation.

Relief flooded through me. I knew that when he said, "Okay by me," what he was really saying was, "It is your right to choose."

I continued to share my beliefs and how I felt that my relationship with God was personal and didn't fit within any specific religion. Uncle Jim listened attentively, offering words of acceptance, guidance, and love.

Leaving that lunch, I felt a weight lifted off my shoulders. I had trusted my inner voice to speak up. My family had accepted me for who I truly was, even choosing not to be a member of their church. Years later, Uncle Jim would even conduct my wedding in Loose Park despite the fact that we didn't get married in an LDS temple or share their beliefs.

The journey of my faith, which aligned with the passing of my father, was a pivotal one for me. As I walked along this path, I learned to listen to my inner voice, embracing the unique route that was destined for me. With an open heart and youthful optimism, I eagerly faced whatever challenges lay ahead, finding joy in even the simplest moments—such as watching the trees bloom and being reminded of the popcorn song, or stumbling upon unexpected opportunities and choosing my path. It was in my roots, loving family, and humble beginnings that I started to find the power of choice and strength in trusting myself.

As I share these thoughts with you, dear reader, I am reminded of the constant struggle we face to break free from the expectations and labels that society, religion, family, jobs, and geography place on us. These can become a confinement, stifling our own potential as we blindly follow someone else's predestined path for our lives. However, I have come to understand that being an audacious optimist means making a mindful choice—to trust in your own intuition and abilities and envision the best possible outcome even when faced with uncertainty. Choosing optimism is an act of self-trust, and it serves as a strong foundation for shaping your own future.

Audacious Optimism in Action

Deep within each of us lies a complex network of roots, some that we cling to for strength and others that are mere fragments of our past. From a young age, I endured the crushing weight of loss and watched my single mother fight for courage. These experiences, coupled with my deep faith and the freedom to explore different paths, have crafted a strong foundation within me.

You may feel the same, or you may feel completely different! Regardless, we all have roots or beginnings, and it is crucial to strike a balance between honoring them, creating your own unique journey in life, and defining who you are.

Tips on how to choose audacious optimism and forge your own path:

- **Be the illustrator of your story:** Think of your life as a blank canvas, just waiting for you to create something beautiful. Take some time to explore this and answer these questions for yourself: What do you want to paint with your brushstrokes that best represents your dreams, passions, and purpose? How do you see the world around you? Once you can answer these and maybe have even written them out on paper, reflect on what you've discovered and then take intentional actions toward shaping your desired future going forward. Whether it's chasing after a dream job, fostering meaningful relationships, or traveling the world, you have the power to illustrate your own life. Be inquisitive, stay curious, and take on big adventures!

- **Let it shape you, not define you:** What influenced your upbringing, life experiences, financial situation, geographical location, and cultural background? Think about what got you where you are today, because these factors have helped shape you into who you are, but they do not determine your entire identity. The more aware you are of the parts of your life that shaped you, the more capable you are to choose what gets to stay with you on your journey and what you will leave behind. Remember that you have the ability to grow and change. Just as trees adapt to their surroundings, so can you. Stay open-minded and consider different perspectives and ways of living. Be open to continually learning. Select the aspects that resonate with you and use them as building blocks for your unique self. *You* are one of a kind.

- **Build your boundaries:** Boundaries are essential to protecting your time, energy, and overall well-being. It is important to clearly define what you consider acceptable and not acceptable in your life. Saying no, or speaking up, reinforces these boundaries and lets others know where you stand. For instance, if you have designated weekends as your family or personal time, you don't need to say yes to spending time with friends. Even within family relationships, setting boundaries is crucial. The fear of disapproval or rejection can often lead us to take on too much. Remember that saying no does not make you any less valuable or worthy. Prioritize your own needs and don't be afraid to say no to requests that do not align with your values or capabilities.

- **Angels of inspiration:** Inspiration can strike at any time, often when you least expect it. Be open to receiving wisdom from various sources, whether it be a friend's guidance, a child's innocent perspective, a brief interaction with a stranger, or even a simple smile. Take note of those who inspire you and reflect on what qualities they possess. Make an internal log of how their words or actions made you feel. Ask yourself what lessons you learned. Consider how you can incorporate these traits into your own journey and also pass them on to others, eventually becoming an angel to someone else in need.

- **Hope is your birthright:** Having hope is not limited to youth or privileged; it is a fundamental human right. No matter your situation or where you are on your individual life journey, you can choose bold hope and confidence in the minutes, hours, and days to come. Believe in yourself, in your potential, and better days ahead. Let your hope be contagious, connecting to those around you with feelings of compassion, kindness, and motivation. This mindset not only benefits you but has the power to positively affect the lives of those around you as well. Remember, hope is something that no one can take away from you. It lives within you. Close your eyes and repeat to yourself that hope is not passive, it is not wishful thinking; hope is belief. Dare to hope.

Life's journey is unpredictable, and sometimes it can throw blows that hit you right in the heart. Yet mindset remains within your control. As you forge your own path, remind yourself that you have free agency to choose each step, and trust your instincts to do what is best for you. You shape your reality, and you are the mastermind of audacious optimism.

Embrace the Unknown

In the space between certainty and fear lies a key element of audacious optimism—the willingness to embrace the unknown. It is more than just a leap of faith; it involves a fundamental shift in perspective—choosing to see opportunities where others might see risks or even impossible barriers. Stepping forward into these moments promotes a growth mindset, acknowledging that your abilities and intelligence can evolve through hard work and dedication.

Embracing the unknown becomes a proactive approach to problem-solving, propelling you forward instead of paralyzing you in uncertainty. Innovation thrives in these uncharted territories. By fearlessly exploring new ideas and solutions without being held back by fear of failure, you open yourself up to new opportunities.

Life is unpredictable, and the unknown is around every corner. Yet within this vastness lies adaptability—the ability to pivot, adjust, and find our way even when the path ahead is obscured. Embracing the unknown equips you with resilience, allowing you to approach life's twists and turns with mental fortitude and determination. Each challenge builds resilience and strength, shaping you into more capable versions of yourself.

Here are a few ways to consider working on embracing the unknown:

- **Start small:** Set achievable goals that challenge the unknown. It could be as small as a single inch or as long as a full mile—progress is progress (yes, there was a nod to *Fast & Furious* in there). Celebrate every success and let it ignite your drive to keep going.

- **Champion change:** Flexibility is key and take it from a dancer, flexibility has to be practiced. Break free from routines; take a different route to work or try new foods. Change your routine. These incremental shifts may seem minor, but they lay the foundation for adapting to bigger changes down the road.

- **Stay curious:** Curiosity transforms fear into excitement. Ask questions, explore, and remain open to new experiences, even when the situation brings anxious feelings. Stay curious. The unknown opens up opportunities for discovery!

- **Build your network:** It's important to surround yourself with a supportive network of friends, family, and mentors who not only encourage you but also help you grow. I often find that when I look around me, I am reminded that I am surrounded by incredible, intelligent, and resilient individuals. Also, engage with people from different backgrounds and experiences. Their insights broaden our understanding and acceptance of the unknown, enhancing our own perspectives.

Embracing the unknown doesn't mean denying your fears, risks, or difficulties. It means believing in your ability to overcome whatever challenges the future may bring. This empowers you to fully live your life with hope, confidence, and determination to handle anything that comes your way—and to follow your North Star.

3

North Star

Everything changed in the weeks following my dad's passing. I was stepping into the unknown: a life without my dad, our early mornings together, his laughter, his smile, his encouragement and strength. My mom was maybe struggling the most.

I remember tiptoeing past my mom's bedroom door, the soft glow of morning light filtering through the curtains. The smell of her eucalyptus lotion lingered in the air as she slept soundly, not stirring until 10, 11, or sometimes 12 in the afternoon on her days off. Those moments were precious to her, a respite from the busy and demanding life of a single parent. Thanks to the small pension she received from the government for my father, she was able to stay home with us for a couple days each week for a short time. It was a comfort to know she was there.

She worked as a licensed practical nurse (LPN) at a local doctor's office, wading in sadness and fatigue to make it through her shifts during the week before taking off three days to care for us. She probably would have stayed in bed if she could, but she knew this grace period of support was fleeting; bills wouldn't pay themselves. Before my dad passed, she was also a high-energy aerobics instructor. After he died, she did this for a while, but eventually withdrew from it, spending her days off sleeping and trying to gather enough strength to give us even a fraction of the attention she used to give before. I always loved seeing her in front of the room counting out the beats like she was Jane Fonda, leotard and all. She was the reason I loved to dance.

During that time, other parts of my mother's behavior began to change. She would often forget important things, such as helping us with schoolwork, paying the bills on time, or even making us dinner—she was overwhelmed and in desperate need of mental health help. Jobs became a source of stress as she struggled to show up on time after helping us get to school or oversleeping or calling in sick often. I couldn't understand why she seemed so tired all the time, why she didn't do more around the house or for herself. As a child, I grew frustrated with her lack of energy and motivation. Even though my mind told me to be patient and understanding, my ambitious personality pushed me to want more from her and the world around me. I wanted my mom to wake up! It wasn't until years later that I learned about her severe depression and breakdowns. Despite a paralyzed mental state, she continued to get out of bed every day solely for us. She was as brave as she could be and did the very best she could.

Every room in our house carried a piece of my dad. His tools scattered in the garage, his favorite chair in the living room, his dark blue bath robe in his bedroom, and even his old leather jacket hanging in the front closet. Yet, the memories were hardest to escape—the smell of freshly cut grass after he mowed the lawn, the laughter from Halloween parties he hosted, and the feeling of his hand holding mine. In the months since his passing, our home felt empty and lifeless without him. Almost as if it was dying with my dad. I found myself hunting for hope, refusing to let sadness consume me.

My dad had always been a dreamer, a doer, and he instilled that same spirit in me. I remembered his words that life is about having enough courage to always try, and I held onto that as I pushed forward with my own dreams. While moments of sadness still hit me like a wave, I also recalled the happy memories and used them to fuel my determination to find happiness again.

My mom tried her best to make that Christmas Eve in 1989 just as magical as it had always been for me and my brothers. She struggled financially after supporting my dad through years of doctor's appointments, failed treatments, and gaps in insurance. She was emotionally and physically exhausted. Yet, even through her overwhelming sadness, my mom made Christmas beautiful.

Thinking back on the first Christmas Eve without my dad, as we all headed to bed the candles flickered and the Christmas tree glistened with classic silver icicles. I couldn't wait to open the presents under the tree. Even if they were only socks, they were wrapped to perfection, beautiful in so many ways and for so many reasons.

My dad and I had been the only early risers in my family. We would sneak out of the house at the break of dawn and he would take me to truck stops for early morning hot coffee (mine, of course, was hot chocolate). He would say, "Waking up early is the first step to achieving greatness."

Then he would give me one of his charming winks and a huge grin.

I remembered those moments that Christmas morning when I woke up at five. I crept downstairs, secretly hoping I would catch Santa Claus slipping presents underneath the tree. I didn't catch him, of course, but smiled and giggled at the extra presents he'd left for us (thank you, Mom). I tiptoed into the kitchen to make myself some hot chocolate complete with a candy cane.

As I sat quietly on the couch next to the glowing Christmas tree sipping hot chocolate, I looked out the window. My whole life I had heard stories about this bright star that played an important role in our faith. I pulled back the white sheers to get a glimpse of this star.

I sipped on my delicious hot chocolate, the warmth spreading through my chest, and gazed up at the clear winter sky. As if on cue, a bright light caught my eye, and I stared at its twinkling and dancing appearance. I couldn't believe it, *there it was!* A bright, magical, and beautiful star that seemed to sparkle just for me. That was it. It had to be real! That was the Christmas star. That was the great guiding light—the North Star!

An uncontrollable grin spread across my face, and I leaned closer to the window, nearly spilling my hot chocolate onto the couch. My whole body was buzzing with excitement at the promise of this breathtaking star, and I knew without a doubt that I would follow it wherever it may lead.

Now, what I actually saw was a half-broken street lamp flickering in and out on the lawn of the apartments across the street. My child mind saw something different. I saw something beautiful, full of opportunity, pointing me in the right direction.

That night I felt a spark ignite within me. It was like a small flame, flickering in the darkness of my world. A world defined by broken streetlamps and the challenges and sadness that seemed to surround us at every turn. It was at that moment that I decided my world would not be shaped by these external forces but rather by my own choices, voice, and determination.

As I watched my mother navigate the world as a single parent, working hard and fighting to make ends meet, my admiration for her grew. Even if she didn't see herself this way, I saw that she was a force to be reckoned with. Despite the hardships we faced, she pushed forward for us.

Even when we had to file for bankruptcy and rely on the church pantry for groceries, my mother never gave up. She remained steadfast in her belief that we could overcome any obstacle thrown our way, even if she had to sleep for a few days first. During all this, she had me—an ambitious, determined daughter who was unaware of social restraints and loved to dance.

When I was 10, a year after my dad died, my mother nervously approached the local dance studio behind the bowling alley in our small town. The building was old and run-down, but inside it was filled with energy and passion. Standing outside, my mother mustered up the courage to ask the cigarette-smoking dance teacher whether I could take lessons, knowing full well that she couldn't pay for them. I can only imagine how embarrassing that moment was for her. What I saw was bravery and determination. I saw a mother seeking opportunities for her daughter—trusting her own instinct to try even if she felt her voice was small.

Rather than simply asking for free lessons, though, my mother presented an idea—that I could work at the studio in exchange for lessons. So, starting then and throughout different points for the next several years when my mom couldn't afford the lessons, I washed mirrors, swept floors, and danced with a newfound appreciation for hard work and determination. This experience taught me that anything is possible. That even in the face of adversity, we can trust ourselves and just speak up and try.

A few years after my mom enrolled me in dance classes, our school announced junior high cheerleading tryouts. As I was transitioning from seventh grade to eighth grade and moving up to junior high, this was a big deal for me. I wanted it so badly! Junior high didn't have a dance team, and since I knew I couldn't audition for the high school dance team until later, I figured cheerleading would be the next best thing. As I prepared for tryouts, I felt I was at a disadvantage. All the other girls also wanted to make the team, especially the popular, thin, and wealthy ones.

Back in the 90s, cheerleading had a stereotypical image, and appearance played a significant role. It was all about looking the part. It didn't matter whether you were coordinated if you had the perfect hair and body. Unfortunately, I didn't fit that mold— let's just say I wasn't exactly the poster child for preteen coolness. I had physically matured earlier than most of my peers, and I was overly smiley and awkward, to say the least.

Despite all of this, none of it mattered to me when it came to trying out for cheerleading. It felt as if every girl in school showed up for tryouts that day. I sat with my neighborhood friend, Lindsay, who was tiny and adorable. I knew she would make it. Surprisingly enough, I remember being more excited about just giving it a shot than making the team. Showing up felt like a win for me!

As the tryouts began, I could feel my heart pounding in my chest. The judges called me up, and I confidently chanted, "Those Jays are dynamite, those Jays are dynamite, those Jays go tick, tick, tick, tick, tick, tick, BOOM, dynamite!" With each word, I kicked higher and did a cartwheel and splits with ease. A smile stretched across my face as I finished the routine. I didn't know whether I had nailed it, but I stuck the landing—with a big smile.

After the tryout, Lindsay's mom picked us up and dropped me off at home. Bursting with excitement, I ran inside to tell my mom all about it. That night, the list of the eighth grade cheerleading team would be posted on the school doors. Despite feeling proud of myself already, I felt nervous about seeing the list and not having my name on it. However, around 7 p.m., Lindsay and her mom came rushing over to my house. She had a paper with all the names of the eighth grade cheerleading team. And there it was—my name was on that list!

A surge of pure youthful joy bubbled up inside me, and I couldn't stop grinning. All my hard work and dedication had paid off, and I swear I could hear Madonna's "Just Like a Prayer" blasting in the background. I was seriously freaking out! I couldn't believe it. Seeing my name on that list felt like a form of winning that I hadn't experienced yet. It solidified the importance to me of believing in myself, just showing up even when I feel like the underdog, and giving it my all no matter the odds.

The start of eighth grade was my turning point. It was a time of pure youthful bliss, where every beat of life seemed to echo my own aspirations.

My growing confidence pushed me to want more. More than the confines of our modest home with its chipped paint. My mom did her best to temper these desires with realistic expectations, but I always pushed for more. I would find a way to make it possible, whether it meant finding the money, the solution, or having the courage to speak up and invite myself to the table.

During this time, three girls became my closest companions—Shea, Laura, and Nikki. Shea exuded an elegant southern charm with her red-golden locks and dazzling smile, and her unwavering faith was an inspiration to us all. Laura, with her quick wit and loyalty, always kept us laughing with her therapist parents' influence evident in her quirky personality. And then there was fiery Italian beauty Nikki, with her sassy attitude and the most infectious laugh. Together, we were a force to be reckoned with—cheering and dancing on the field and spending countless hours together off the field. Of course, like any sisterhood, we had our fair share of arguments and fights, but in the end, our bond was thick. We always found a way to work through any teenage drama. Our friendship was built on genuine connection.

As a typical teenager, I couldn't help but compare what I had and what I didn't have. Whenever I visited *any* of my other friends' homes, I felt envious. Our own humble house seemed insignificant in comparison: always cluttered, with various broken items scattered about and my mother's increasing obsession with cats. At one point, we had nine felines roaming around in that tiny space. One of them, Chloe, even had a habit of chewing on clothes. If I left a shirt on my bed or the floor, I would later find it with gaping holes and kitty teeth marks. Our home was an awkward situation that embarrassed me at times. However, my friends Shea, Laura, and Nikki never made me feel ashamed of where I lived, no matter how different it was from their homes. They helped me embrace the fact that my life looked different and that was okay; it was just a part of my story. They loved my mom like any best friends should, and they didn't hesitate to come over even if I tried avoiding it. Even Laura, despite her allergies to cats, would brave through the discomfort just to make sure I felt included. They taught me important lessons about accepting myself, being proud of where I came from, and not letting my mess define me.

When I turned 16, I didn't have the privilege of owning a car. But that was okay; by then, I had made enough friends that someone was always willing to pick me up. Sometimes it would be my boyfriend, other times it would be my buddies Jason and Scott.

I absolutely loved it every time Jason picked me up in his sleek silver Probe—that car personified the 90s!

Then one morning my mom and brothers surprised me by saying they had a gift for me. When I looked outside, there sat an old beat-up gray Plymouth. I couldn't believe it. Was this really for me? My mom and brothers beamed at me, nodding their heads in confirmation. I ran up to the car, examining every inch of it. The paint was chipped in some places, ceiling fabric falling off, and there were dents here and there. It was in bad shape to say the least, but I just didn't care. It was a gift of independence. I didn't have to try to find rides everywhere anymore. I had my own. This was my freedom!

Throughout that year, I continued to build on my ambitious momentum. My mom continued to remind me to be cautious about dreaming too big because she wanted to be able to catch me or help me if I fell short. However, through the worried lens built by years of pain, I know she admired my determination and tenacity, which were on full display on the day I was crowned Prom Queen. As my mom looked over at one of my high school teachers, Mr. Brown, he said to her, "She's dynamite, Reina. She's a force to be reckoned with, not an underdog, and she's always going to find her way, especially with that determination of hers."

By the end of my high school career, my goals seemed clear: secure a spot at a prestigious university complete with a dance scholarship. That was the ticket to my dreams! I was confident and ready to face the challenges of making this dream come true—that is, until mononucleosis hit. Yes, dreaded mono, at 18 years old. The timing couldn't have been worse; I was bedridden right before the scheduled big college auditions, and I missed them. I was crushed.

Then something magical happened. Without my knowledge, my shy yet resourceful mom took matters into her own hands. She approached a nearby liberal arts college that she had begged me to apply to, and I was accepted—William Jewell College. She spoke with the dance coaches and secured an audition on my behalf. In lieu of a live performance, they watched a compilation of my dance highlights on VHS. Yes, my mother convinced them to roll out a TV with a VCR. She popped in the tape and auditioned for me. Their decision? They awarded me a place on the team and a scholarship. My mom had made the college dance team for me. This opportunity coupled with other scholarships, support from a group of my high school teachers, and financial aid made my dream of college a reality.

My mom didn't always have the strongest voice, but still many times throughout my life I saw her use it, even when she felt weak, and take action when she felt paralyzed by sadness and fear and all she wanted to do was go back to bed. Her strength had carved a clear albeit winding path to a world overflowing with opportunities. Our physical home may have been falling apart, but my mom's spirit fought to not completely break, which kept our family strong. She held out her hand often, not out of weakness, but as a symbol of desire to overcome challenges that came our way. Each step she took was a courageous leap of faith, and she walked through the unknown, driven by sometimes desperate hope, but hope nonetheless.

Audacious Optimism in Action

I often think back to that Christmas morning when a broken streetlamp became my North Star. In that moment, I made the decision to see past the obstacles and find beauty in imperfection. It was a valuable lesson that has stayed with me, reminding me that I always have the power to choose how I view the world and uncover opportunities.

Life can be chaotic and it's not always easy to see a guiding light in place of a broken streetlamp. The brokenness may seem overwhelming at times. However, no matter how hard it may be, try to see more. See the opportunity.

Tips on how to choose audacious optimism and find beauty in the brokenness:

- **Gratitude reflection:** Take a moment each day to pause and reflect on the things you are grateful for, even the smallest of blessings. Let your mind wander to moments of joy, shifting your focus from any feelings of brokenness to a sense of thankfulness, even if it is just being thankful for simply waking up or having that cup of coffee. Find something to say, "I am grateful for this." This act of gratitude will guide you toward a feeling of hope, even in the darkest of moments.

- **Shift the lens:** When confronted with challenges, intentionally shift your point of view and consider different angles. Instead of seeing difficulties as roadblocks, ask yourself: "What can I gain from this situation?" or "In what ways could this challenge help me grow?" By changing the lens through which you view adversity, you open yourself up to opportunities for learning and self-improvement.

- **Seek beauty in imperfection:** Embrace the beauty in the imperfect world that surrounds you. It's often found in unexpected places, like an old hoodie that holds sentimental value, a garden with wild growth but delicious tomatoes, or a house with chipped paint that still feels like home. When we view imperfections as unique traits, they become part of our personal stories and shape who we are. Finding beauty in these imperfections transforms them from blemishes to cherished imprints on our lives, each one adding depth and character to our stories.

- **Ask and offer:** Truly engage in meaningful interactions with others by approaching them with empathy and actively listening to their words without solely focusing on your response. When you do this, you will find that people are more willing to assist you when you need it most. And when you do ask for help, guidance, or introductions, remember that it's not just about taking; offer something in return, whether it's your expertise, time, support, or connections. (a nod to Yarrow Kraner, CEO of HATCH).

- **Visualize your North Star:** Envision your ultimate goal, the pinnacle of achievement that you strive toward in any situation. What is it that you aspire to do, accomplish, overcome? Close your eyes and let this vision become your guiding light, a shining North Star that leads you forward. Visualize it every day, allowing its magnetic pull to guide you forward even when the path seems daunting and uncertain. Let it fuel your determination and inspire you to keep pushing through any obstacles in your way.

Perspective is up to you—a lens through which you interpret the world. By practicing audacious optimism, it shapes your perspective and becomes your fuel for resilience—you will find your North Star rather than a broken streetlamp. Now you've started to tap into mental toughness.

Mental Toughness

Within the depths of your mind, where aspirations and ambitions hang out, there exists a phrase that holds power: "I will." These two simple words are not merely statements; they are agents of change, architects of destiny, and anchors of mental toughness.

When you vocalize "I will," you move beyond passively wishing for something. You cast off uncertainty and put on the armor of determination. It's as if the universe leans in, recognizing your resolve, and whispers, "Very well, let it be so!"

Confidence is sparked in those who use this phrase. It's not arrogance; it's the belief that challenges can be overcome, dreams can be realized, and obstacles can be conquered. With each "I will," you claim ownership over your future and boldly believe it will unfold according to your vision.

"I will" ignites a fire within you and is fueled by trusting your inner voice and having faith in your abilities. This fire does not flicker; it roars—a guiding light through uncertainty, doubt, and adversity. The confidence ignited by this fire may seem audacious, and it is. It is bold to believe in yourself, and it is a risk you must take!

It is also not limited to individuals alone. Families, teams, entire companies, groups, even communities can embrace this mental toughness. When "I will" becomes "we will," a shared determination to achieve a vision becomes the fuel for progress, growth, and success.

It all starts with a choice and the longing to confidently envision a brighter future. Let "I will" become your mental toughness mantra, your way forward. For within those two words lies the potential for goal-exceeding transformation.

How to put your "I WILL" to work daily:

- **Commit to yourself:** Start declaring, "I will!" Say aloud, "I will overcome challenges," or "I will make progress today," or "I will work out today." This becomes a promise to yourself—a commitment.

  Let's try it. What can you put "I will" in front of right now? These things can be daily to-do's or big dreams—the intentions are yours.

  I will _____

  I will _____

  I will _____

- **Remove limiting words:** By eliminating words such as "should," "could," and "would," you empower yourself. These words imply uncertainty or hesitation. Replace them with "I WILL!" This audacious shift in language propels you toward action and conviction.

- **Future as present:** When discussing your goals, speak as if they're already yours. Visualize success and embrace it. Confidently declaring your intentions is like staking a claim to your future.

- **Visual reminders:** Write down your intentions. Sticky notes, phone reminders, or a journal can reinforce your commitment. My personal favorite is the sticky note (thank you, design thinking)!

Feel the power of your mental toughness, a force that fuels your relentless determination like a champion athlete. Channel your inner strength, and let it surge through your mind and body, propelling you forward with focus and resilience—believe in yourself.

Personally, my mental toughness was shaped and refined as a professional athlete for the NFL.

Champion Spirit

always loved being on stage and connecting with an audience. In high school, I was the 1998 conference champion for a dramatic interpretation called *A Piece of My Heart*, a powerful, true drama of six women who went to Vietnam to entertain the troops. I gravitated to these women's boldness and their magnetic personalities. I loved the act of living out their experiences to convey the important message to help others.

It wasn't just the stage I loved—it was connecting with and inspiring people through storytelling. I graduated from William Jewell College in the early 2000s with a degree in communication. I interned at the local NBC affiliate with aspirations to become a news anchor just like my career idol Katie Couric.

As fate would have it, my passion for storytelling took an unexpected turn. Instead of pursuing a career in television, I found myself working for a corporate pediatric nonprofit. Here, I used my ability to craft compelling narratives to share with donors and supporters about the incredible impact their donations were making in the lives of children in need. I can still hear the words of our founder, Jeanne Lillig-Patterson, echoing in my head, "You don't need to be in front of the camera to be a storyteller. Your words have the power to change lives anywhere at any time."

Each day, I sat in my small corner of a sprawling campus in Kansas City, centered on a magnificent spire that seemed to reach up to the clouds—etched with binary code in the shape of the DNA double helix. It was a powerful reminder that I was part of something much bigger than myself at the intersection of health care, technology and philanthropy.

My colleagues at the office affectionately dubbed me "The Cheerleader" for my vibrant and enthusiastic personality. So, it was fitting when I became an actual NFL cheerleader for the greatest team in football, the Kansas City Chiefs. It was a dream come true when, out of hundreds of hopefuls, I was only one of six rookies welcomed onto the team.

Stepping into the auditions that year at the Chiefs, practice facility, I immediately sensed that this talent was next level. It was impressive and intimidating. My eyes scanned the room, taking in the glimmer of perfectly coordinated outfits. These were the best of the best.

I felt a wave of uncertainty wash over me. I took a deep breath to calm my nerves, almost as if I could breathe in and trap all of the fear and doubt. With each step forward, I felt the weight of my worn-out sports bra bearing my alma mater's nickname, "Jewell," across my chest. To be honest, I was feeling a bit more like a crumpled napkin than a shiny jewel.

Looking around at the sea of talented candidates, I closed my eyes and reminded myself of all the hard work and sacrifices that had led me to this moment. A memory of my mother's courageous support flashed through my mind as I whispered to myself, "You worked too hard to walk away. Mom worked too hard for you to walk away. You can do this. You will do it!" Opening my eyes, I exhaled that trapped breath, releasing confident determination. I was ready.

During the interview portion, my soon-to-be coach greeted me with a warm and playful smile, "Well, hello there, Jewell."

Despite knowing it wasn't my given name, she said they had given me the nickname during judging. Then she asked, "What inspired you to become an NFL cheerleader for the greatest team in football?" I gave her a big smile and dove into my response.

For the next three days, I gave those auditions everything I had. All the years I had poured into dance came pouring out of me in pure and expressive joy.

I left the practice facility after three grueling days of auditions, exhausted and emotional in the best way. My body ached from hours of dancing, but my heart was full. I had poured everything I had onto that dance floor, leaving nothing behind.

Whether I made the team or not, I knew I had given it my all and met some amazing people along the way.

Two days later, as I anxiously scanned the list of names posted on the Chiefs website, my heart nearly exploded when I read: **Shanna, 2003 Kansas City Chiefs Cheerleader – Rookie.**

I was a Kansas City Chiefs CHEERLEADER! I couldn't help but think back to all those years of choreographing routines in my basement, joining my mom at aerobic classes, and finally getting to take dance lessons.

The moment I had been eagerly awaiting had finally arrived. After being warmly welcomed onto the team by the seasoned veterans and forming bonds with my fellow rookies, it was time for us to take the field for our very first game.

As the sun slowly crept over the horizon on that highly anticipated pregame morning in late summer, I drove to the stadium, heart racing with excitement. It felt like a dream.

I finally caught my first glimpse of the stadium—the sunlight seemed to perfectly surround it with a golden glow, as if even nature recognized the significance of this team. Indeed, it was a kingdom filled with legendary athletes and loyal fans ready to cheer them on.

The scent of sizzling tailgate barbecue drifted through the air. This was my very first NFL game day experience. The excitement bubbling within me was almost too much to contain.

Stepping into the locker room was like walking into a different world of red and gold. My Chiefs-branded bag hung from my shoulder as I unpacked my belongings and hung up my uniform in my designated locker. I quickly changed into my practice attire and grabbed my poms, following the veterans out onto the field like an eager puppy to start the pregame practice!

Although we had tirelessly rehearsed for this day, nothing could compare to the feeling of preparing to perform on game day. With my heart pounding in anticipation, I ran out to the east end zone alongside four of my fellow rookies—Cat, Amy, Lindsay, and

Shauntel. We looked at each other and shared a moment of smiles that reached our eyes in silent celebration.

As we huddled together, Shauntel couldn't help but comment, "I am so happy you got your eyebrows waxed, Shan (her nickname for me). Now you look game ready, and I can tell you actually have two." We all burst out laughing—no one louder than Lindsay—feeling a sense of camaraderie and excitement. Our coach's voice broke through our chatter as she instructed us to get into formation.

As our first early-morning game day field practice came to an end (cheerleaders, just like players, warm up and practice before the game), I hit the final pose of our dance routine with a beaming smile. This moment was everything to me. We quickly made our way inside the locker room, trying to ignore the towering figures of the football players darting past us on their way to practice. Eeek! I couldn't be more excited, and I knew I was ready for my first game. The next hour of getting game day ready was a blur of adrenaline and the scent of hair products. Red lips, check! Red nails, check! Poms, check!

It was game time!

As I held onto my poms tightly, slipped into my sleek white high-heeled boots, and let my hair fall into perfect waves around my shoulders, I couldn't believe I was here at this very moment.

Stepping back onto the field, the sound was unlike anything I had ever experienced before. My jaw dropped in awe as a veteran cheerleader walked up beside me and said with a wink, "Pretty amazing right? And to think this is just preseason. Just wait until our first regular season home game. Your ears will be ringing for weeks. It's an unbelievable feeling."

With a knowing grin, she added, "Now shake those poms. The intro is about to start!"

The roar of the crowd filled my ears as the game continued, each second bringing more energy and excitement into the stadium.

I danced with pure joy to the beat of "Start Me Up" by the Rolling Stones, losing myself in the euphoria of the moment. Even as sweat dripped down my face, my energy and smile never faltered.

A veteran cheerleader had advised me to take a moment to look up at the highest point of the stadium and envision dancing so big and energetically that the fans up top could see me. I followed her advice and gazed up at the towering structure, which neared the clouds, and did just that. As I was dancing, the thought crossed my mind that my dad would have loved to see this, and it brought happy tears. I took in the immense feeling of joy and pride in that moment. I sent up a burst of gratitude toward Heaven. Surrounded by thousands of cheering fans and my teammates, who were becoming like family, there was no place else I'd rather be. Being a cheerleader, for this team, with these athletes, felt like home.

After the first year, I came back and auditioned again, and again, and again. Each time coming back with a fire that was greater than the year before because I knew just how much there was to lose. Every year, the team was filled with incredible individuals—strong, athletic, and fiercely loyal to one another. In the face of defeat or seemingly impossible challenges, our smiles never wavered. It was more than just a game for us, it was ingrained in every fiber of our being.

Cheerleading was not just our sport; it was a way of life that we embraced wholeheartedly with passion and determination. And we wore those qualities proudly as we worked tirelessly to elevate each other and our team to new heights.

Throughout my time with the team, I had the privilege of cheering for what could be argued as the best team in the entire NFL. I stood on the sidelines and cheered for some of the greatest players to ever grace the field: Trent Green with his pinpoint accuracy, Priest Holmes with his unstoppable speed and agility, Tony Gonzalez with his catches and touchdowns,

Eric Berry with his fierce determination, Jamaal Charles with his lightning-fast moves, Dante Hall with his electrifying kick returns, and many other incredible athletes. Despite occasional moments when the seats in the stadium were not filled in the fourth quarter, our spirits never broke on the sidelines as we formed lifetime bonds and made unforgettable memories. The energy and intensity among us were always ablaze, ignited by our passion for the game and loyalty to each other.

The memories with my teammates during my eight seasons are etched into my mind like a beautiful, glittering mosaic. I can still feel the adrenaline pumping through my veins each time I pulled on those crisp, white knee-high boots and donned that sparkling uniform. The roar of the frenzied Kansas City crowd filled my ears as I stepped onto the field, every chant and cheer fueling my pride and passion—that never got old. Amid all the glory and excitement of being a professional cheerleader, it was the refinement that came from expert coaching that truly defined my career.

Under the guidance of our beloved coach, each practice was a test of our strength and endurance, knowledge of game day routines, commitment to our sport and to each other. She was a phenomenal leader and held us to high standards, constantly pushing us to reach our full potential with a blend of assertiveness, expert guidance, athletic experience, and motivation.

Through her tireless training, we evolved from individual dancers into a solid team of elite athletes; a family bound by fierce devotion, and a great love for our sport. The hours spent in the Chiefs practice facility were long, and they were some of the most transformative years of my life. My body had become strong, but it was my mind that had truly undergone a metamorphosis—developing the resilience and champion spirit of a professional athlete; more than just positivity, it's the unbreakable determination to not just say "I'll try," but to boldly declare, "I will" and push myself through every practice and all of the training. This was not because my body always wanted to but rather because my mental fortitude had become stronger than any physical limitations, and my commitment to excellence— saying "I will"—was an unspoken promise I made to my coach, team, and, most importantly, to myself.

Each practice and game day also brought its own lesson, instilling values of resilience and perseverance. These lessons shaped not only my athletic abilities but also my professional career and personal character in the years to come. I refined my inner strength and determination through dedication to my sport and team; I found my voice as a leader among my team- mates. It taught me to value the support of others and constantly strive for improvement, rather than settling for the status quo and average results. As we pushed through some of the most dif- ficult practices and tough games, I learned the power of perse- verance even under the pressure of a possible loss—with a basic facial expression of raising my eyebrows—a small gesture that maintained a smile on my face even when my muscles burned, sweat poured down my back, and my team might be about to feel the agony of defeat. It was the outward expression of me willing myself to keep going.

The most memorable moments and games seemed to always be intertwined with the ever-changing Midwest weather. While cheering on our team and braving the elements at a late summer or early fall game, we had to embrace the extremes of our climate.

Even during rain-soaked games, as my wet hair slapped against my face with every turn, I couldn't help but sport a wide smile and kick extra high, despite mascara running down my cheeks. Believe me, cheerleaders know how to dance with pure joy during a downpour—a great metaphor for life. It was all part of the game day experience in the Midwest—unpredictable and exhilarating.

As a member of the team for eight seasons, I also had the honor of being chosen as team captain for six consecutive seasons (2005–2011). My dedication and hard work on the field paid off when I was selected as a Pro Bowl cheerleader in 2007. This prestigious opportunity allowed me to not only showcase my talents but to also represent the Chiefs proudly on a national level in beautiful Hawaii at the Pro Bowl Game.

One of my most cherished memories from this experience was lining up for the football player run through with the warm ocean breeze tousling my hair. As I excitedly hit every pose, I caught sight of Chiefs legend Tony Gonzalez sprinting toward us and into our tunnel. Now, looking back on that moment, he embodied the real-life version of Maui from Disney's *Moana*, and his larger-than-life energy and smile were infectious. He pointed directly at me as he ran past and exclaimed, "That's our KC girl!" I couldn't help but beam with pride and gratitude for being part of such an incredible team.

I loved every minute on the field, and my involvement with the military appreciation tours held a special place in my heart. Alongside 12 fellow Chiefs cheerleaders, from 2005 to 2011 we toured to different locations in the world visiting U.S. military bases and delivering a two-hour variety show that paid tribute to America's history from 1940 to 2000.

My personal performance highlight was my impersonation of the one and only Elvis Presley, complete with his iconic hip shake! I likely didn't reach the charisma of Austin Butler's portrayal on screen, but I certainly gave it my all. Our touring team was like a real-life version of *Pitch Perfect*—brimming with singing, dancing, deep friendships, and a lot of fun along the way (minus the Hollywood glamour and a capella mash-up competitions).

Our travels included locations such as Guantanamo Bay, the Sinai Peninsula, Egypt, Portugal, Honduras, and El Salvador. The constant movement and adventure was exhilarating, and the purpose behind our travels made all the extra-long practices (in addition to the game day practices, appearances, and the actual game days), flights, questionable food, and body aches worth it. The world became a little bigger. We were always greeted with the most amazing NFL, and specifically Chiefs, fans no matter where we went, and we pushed ourselves to deliver the best performance we had in us at every single location. We relied on lots of coffee and the tired laughter we constantly shared—we loved every minute of it.

The positive energy we radiated spread like glitter, and the smiles on the service men and women's faces made it all worth it. We brought them a little piece of something they loved so much from home—nostalgic memories through the music of our performances, and of course . . . NFL football! It truly was a magical time filled with laughter, friendship, and memories I will never forget.

The travel was exciting and meaningful, but my true love of being part of the Chiefs was being at Arrowhead. There was nothing like being on that legendary field. I experienced the roller coaster of emotions that encompassed both exhilarating highs and devastating lows—even though I was a cheerleader and knew how to keep a smile on my face, I was still a fan and felt the game outcome with the team. Through each victory and defeat, the cheerleaders always stood as one, united by our love for the game and our commitment as athletes to our sport.

The thrill of a well-deserved win taught us to raise our voices above the roar of the crowd and push forward with determination and excitement, and even more so if we went into overtime. We shook our poms, danced with precision, and kicked to our faces repeatedly, as the anticipation of the approaching win pulsed through our veins.

In those tough games where the outcome seemed uncertain or bleak, we found strength in our camaraderie—smiling at each other from across the field or in our cheer groups with that look that seemed to say, "We got this."

We were each other's biggest cheerleaders thanks to our coach's unifying guidance—it was invaluable. We held tight to the lessons we learned in leadership and how to look to our teammates on either side and trust in their abilities and commitment to complement our own. We worked to be better than we thought we could be with each practice and game day, strengthening our physical performance and our mental toughness.

As the years passed, my time as a professional cheerleader came to an inevitable end in 2011—eight seasons, 89 games, and 8750 hours perfecting my sport—with tears of joy, I hung up my pom poms and walked off the field for the last time, bidding farewell to a chapter of my life that overflowed with love and friendships that will last a lifetime.

As the current head coach of the Kansas City Chiefs, Andy Reid, has said and stamped on the very heart of GEHA Field at Arrowhead Stadium, "Walk in as teammates, leave as family."

The fire that ignited within me during those exhilarating games will forever burn bright in my heart. The field-born energy and champion spirit—determination, perseverance, hard work, and willpower—that my days as a professional athlete refined are imprinted on my very soul.

I will always be a cheerleader.

Audacious Optimism in Action

Audacious optimism and an athlete's champion mindset are closely connected through mental toughness. Athletes exhibit resilience, handle pressure, visualize success, maintain focus and adaptability, and persevere during training, competitions, and recovery. Whether in sports or life, cultivating these attitudes leads to greatness.

However, being an athlete isn't a prerequisite for activating this mindset. It's about identifying your goal, passion, or vision unapologetically, whether you're just starting out or embarking on a new chapter. You hold the power to achieve remarkable things and live out your dreams. Believe it!

Tips on how to choose audacious optimism and activate a champion mindset:

- **Be your own cheerleader:** Grab your poms and face fear and doubt with audacity by believing in yourself—whether at a young age or later in life, you are never too old to be a cheerleader for your damn self! Make a firm declaration of "I will," and watch as you overcome challenges and setbacks along the way. Your commitment to excellence is a silent promise you make to yourself—you are your own biggest cheerleader! And once you believe in yourself, you will authentically and loudly cheer on others as well.

- **Expect the unpredictable:** The ability to be flexible and adapt is essential. Expect that change will come and embrace it with an open mind, adjusting your approach as circumstances shift. Like cheerleaders who dance happily in the pouring rain, face life's unpredictability with enthusiasm and curiosity. As we are well aware, change is a constant, and it will require resilience, adaptability, and strength to overcome any situation, even those that may feel like defeat. It's all part of the thrilling experience of the journey you are on.

- **Identify and invest in your team:** It is crucial to consciously prioritize the team surrounding you each and every day. Your team can encompass a wide range of people, from friends made later in life to childhood friends, sports teams, family members, coworkers, neighbors, and beyond. These connections, built on loyalty, commitment, shared experiences, and common goals, are vital components of life. Take a moment to appreciate the people in your life once a day. Yes, once a day reach out to someone by text, write a thank-you note, send an encouraging email, or simply call and tell someone you appreciate them. Gratitude strengthens bonds; and when interacting with those people who you consider your team, put away distractions. Give them your full attention. Whether it's a stop by to see your aging parents, a quick drop in on a friend, a virtual meeting, or a coffee break, be present in the moment.

- **Bring big authentic energy (BAE):** Strip away the facade and show your true, authentic self. Be unapologetically vulnerable and let your flaws and struggles be seen. Start tapping into your BAE by understanding your strengths, values, and passions. Write them down. Get to know what a badass you are. When you're actually aware of what makes you unique, you can confidently and boldly express yourself. And this isn't just a benefit to you. Genuinely share this energy with those around you—particularly your chosen team. Whether you're officially a leader or just a friend, this big authentic energy inspires others. Show who you are, and own every imperfection that made you precious and unique!

- **Do it the "Chiefs' way":** The "Chiefs' way" represents a fierce determination that can extend beyond the football field. The Chiefs build upon their successes, using momentum to drive even more positive outcomes. In life, it's important to recognize when things are going well and use that energy to propel yourself forward. The Chiefs refuse to settle for mediocrity; they have their sights set on victory and are fierce in their pursuit. This same mindset should be applied in your own journey—be bold, be edgy, be audacious, and don't settle for the status quo! So take a page from their playbook and pursue your goals with determination, heart, and mental toughness.

You are the champion of your story; leverage audacious optimism, tap into your mental toughness, and keep pushing toward your win!

Health Journey Begins

My walk in life has led me to discover audacious optimism, which begins with a mindful choice, trusting yourself, embracing the unknown, and tapping into mental toughness. These aren't mere words or phrases; rather, they are a compass, or North Star, and fuel for a daily practice.

I once believed optimism sprang from happiness, success, or seeking opportunity. But optimism is much more profound than that—it is the choice that precedes all else. It wasn't until I embarked on my health journey, where I felt as if the darkness was enveloping my physical and mental state, that I truly grasped the audacious act of choosing optimism—against all odds.

2011: Shanna Land

In the months following my retirement as a cheerleader, I took on a side hustle with the Chiefs in-house production company while also growing as a nonprofit leader. It was an exciting time for me as I had the opportunity to work alongside NFL production legends, pilot a new show called *Red & Gold* specifically for female football fans, interview players, emcee community engagement events, and regularly host auditions for the Chiefs cheerleading team. I even had the opportunities to branch out into other projects such as commercials, guest speaking engagements, and hosting special events.

One unforgettable moment during this time was when I was asked to be one of the emcees for a fan appreciation event for the Kansas City Royals at the Kansas City Power and Light District. The entire Royals team was there, along with hundreds of devoted fans. As a diehard fan of both the Chiefs and Royals (thanks to my dad and older brothers, Erik and Steven), it was an incredible experience to work with both franchises.

Before walking on stage to greet the crowd—a sea of blue—I had an earpiece placed in my left ear by the A/V team so they could feed me speaking cues and information. As soon as I started talking, I noticed that I couldn't hear the crowd properly. *How could that be?* It was as if the microphone was blocking out all other sounds, which seemed strange since it was only in one ear. Acting quickly, I removed the earpiece and relied on visual cues from the crew instead.

For days afterward, I couldn't shake off that bizarre moment on stage. It was exceptionally strange. It bothered me that I hadn't noticed any hearing problems in my left ear before. And every time I thought about it, a strange buzzing sensation would course through my body like a chill—it was trying to tell me something. I couldn't explain it, but something about that experience just felt off and unsettling.

I started to take note of changes in my hearing and general listening mannerisms; for example, I was only using my left ear to talk on the cell phone, or I would ask people several times to repeat what they were saying. If I did use my right ear, I had to have the volume up to the loudest setting. I had a conversation with my friend Cat, a registered nurse, and mentioned to her what happened and that I felt my hearing was decreasing in my right ear. "Oh my gosh, Shanna," she said. "I thought you had just been ignoring me for the past few years. We called it Shanna Land."

I looked at her shocked and said, "What! Who called it Shanna Land?" She responded in her gentle Cat way with, "Ohhh, me, Krissy, Jeron, Linds, Mal, Liz . . . pretty much the whole team."

That got a laugh and a side eye, but also, I was concerned. I had a lot of ear infections that year, so maybe that had damaged my hearing. *Maybe.*

That next week, I scheduled an appointment with my doctor. The clinic was conveniently nestled within the corporate campus, a mere walk away from my desk. As I walked through the familiar corridors, with sleek glass panels and modern furniture, I couldn't help but be proud of the forward-thinking concept behind the clinic: to create a community that revolutionized our experiences with health care. It was a living lab, where we could witness firsthand the cutting-edge technology that our company was developing for electronic health records.

I explained to my doctor about the sudden fullness I felt in my ear and difficult time hearing I had felt during an event I hosted earlier in the week. She conducted a thorough check of my vitals before looking inside my ear canal. After a few moments of examination, she informed me that my right ear appeared mildly irritated and recommended treating it as an inner ear infection with a prescribed antibiotic. She also mentioned that I could be experiencing some minor hearing issues from being exposed to the loudest stadium in the world for so many years.

That seemed reasonable and felt right, until it didn't. Little did I know the twists and turns and upside-down loops my health care journey would take from there.

2012: The Journey Begins

Over the next year, I continued to go back to the doctor. For many visits, I went with symptoms such as fullness in my ear and sinus problems coupled with brain fog and fatigue. The mild hearing loss wasn't really discussed and not something that was a terrible inconvenience at the time. It was just looming in the background. Because my symptoms were related to my ear, sinuses, and sometimes headaches, I was commonly treated for bacterial infections and given a Z-Pak antibiotic or simply instructed to drink water and relax. My doctor talked with me about stress from my busy life, even offering me antianxiety medications just in case.

Maybe I was anxious. Maybe I was just burning the candle at both ends and needed to slow down. *I was too young and healthy for anything to be seriously wrong, right?* Maybe my busy lifestyle was affecting my immune system. Or maybe there was something more. I just felt off, not like a healthy 30-something-year-old.

While my body sent signals, my tried and true inner voice was being slowly overpowered by self-doubt. I had been to the doctor so many times with the same complaint that I started to feel embarrassed to call again.

The more times I visited the doctor, the more I thought, *They think I'm a hypochondriac.*

And that is what I started to believe.

I did not trust my instincts enough in those first years to do what I now know I should have done. The doctors' words became true every time, and that truth was telling me I just needed to change my lifestyle or take another medication. It didn't tell me to request a specialist or get another opinion. Hindsight is 20/20, as the saying goes.

Too many people can relate to this story, both men and women, but especially women because the male body was the standard for health and disease in medical practice and research for decades. Today, we see the impact of this in stories where women are underdiagnosed for heart disease, endometriosis, ADHD, anxiety, and more. I find it fascinating that the word "hysteria" actually originates from the Greek word for "uterus." This has become a deeply rooted subconscious go-to in the medical community that when a woman complains about her health, it is related to a hormonal imbalance or it is all in her head. Hysteria.[1] There has been a gender bias in medicine, and it affects how doctors approach women—often attributing symptoms such as exhaustion, headaches, and anxiety to simply being a woman who has periods, or just being a mom. This happened to me and no one understood me.

During my repeat doctor visits, I started to think maybe this was just my new normal (a new normal before COVID-19, which has become another before-after time in our lives). I was sure my body would adjust, and it did. Our bodies are smart, and mine knew when I was a little off balance on the right to compensate by leaning to the left. Or when I felt a little dizzy or tired, to grab a coffee. Even alcohol. Alcohol of any kind would make me feel normal, until I would wake up with a terrible headache or throw up after having only two drinks. This was my new normal.

My body quickly adjusted to the unfamiliar symptoms, like a diver acclimating to the pressure of deep waters. But as I continued down the path of seeking answers, each doctor's visit and prescription seemed to blur together in a haze of waiting rooms and doctors' orders.

In my eagerness to stay positive and avoid self-doubt, I convinced myself that these antibiotics must be helping—I was fine. I had opened the door to denial, allowing toxic positivity to take root, silencing my instinct to push for answers and hindering my own progress toward true healing.

My instinct was a powerful tool that I pushed aside in favor of a forced smile and being fine.

The doctor-patient relationship is built on trust, so I had no reason to assume my doctor wasn't doing everything possible to figure things out, especially as I returned again and again and again. My inner voice, now a soft whisper, kept nudging me and making my mind swirl. *Was I fine? Or were these constant prescriptions not only masking my physical symptoms but also eroding my self-trust?*

2013: Blinded by Love

In early spring of 2013, I met my husband, Jeff. He asked me on a date after meeting me in a group of mutual friends. We had all just completed the St. Patrick's Day 5 K race in Kansas City.

In fact, he had only participated in the race because two of our friends told him I would be there. He put on all the green he owned to celebrate the holiday and stand out. I found out later that before this race, he hadn't run more than a few blocks for years. In true wooing fashion, he finished the race like a champ.

I thought Jeff was incredibly handsome, and his quirky charm made me smile. I knew enough about him to know he was always the life of the party, successful, and a good person. As we stood there at the Westport Kelly's bar for the traditional post-race beer, he turned to me and said, "I just finished a race for you, in case you didn't know. I am not sure I will be able to move my legs for a few days, but when I can I think the least you could do is go on a date with me."

I told him maybe, and then I said, "Just promise that you will shower before we go because right now you and I both could use one." Now, in *no way* did I mean this as a suggestion, but Jeff's eyes turned instantly mischievous and he jumped on the opportunity, "Ohhhh, yes we do need showers."

Insert my eyes rolling and flaming red cheeks.

Now, obviously this wasn't completely romantic, but it also wasn't a complete failure—it was true to his personality. He laughed at himself and said, "I had to. I couldn't let that opportunity pass."

I laughed too and said, "Okay. Back to the question. A date. Yes to a date."

I really hoped he was a good guy. I had just shared with one of my friends that I knew what I wanted and I was ready to find it—a guy who was funny, self-confident, financially stable, adventurous, loving, and ready to meet a wonderful woman like me. I really didn't think that was too much to ask! Little did I know that same friend was the one who told Jeff I would be running in the race, which is the reason he showed up.

Well played, Matchmaker, well played.

As it turned out, Jeff wasn't just a good guy. He was a great guy! He ticked all the nonnegotiable boxes!

From our first date, over some great wine and flirty exchanges where he promised he would show me the world, we were inseparable. It didn't matter what we were doing, as long as we were doing it together. Even if that meant yard work at his house. Oh yes, Jeff loved yard work dates where he would dish out orders and make me carry the trimmed branches or push the lawnmower. They were romantic dates because they were fun and just the two of us being ourselves.

I loved being around Jeff because he too shared my love for life and adventure, my future-focused way of thinking, and my love for the big-dream conversations.

Our days were filled with breezy fun and laughter as we went on bike rides, runs, long walks, and short weekend trips. It was a natural connection. Jeff's genuine kindness and positive outlook on life mirrored my own, and our spirits were drawn to each other like magnets. Happy attracts happy, and our relationship was like a constant serotonin boost for both of us. It helped me push aside any nagging thoughts that may have crept into my mind, continually trying to remind me that something was wrong with my body.

I was wearing my love glasses, seeing everything through a rosy lens, and it was wonderful. However, as life often goes, plans don't always happen in the order we want them to. And that's okay because they happen in the order they're meant to!

Several months into our romance, we knew two things for certain: we were deeply in love, and we were going to be parents! As this exciting news sank in and took over my initial shock, it gave way to a huge smile. I was going to be a mother! The gravity of the moment swept over me, filling me with an indescribable joy that brought happy tears. This was my family, a unit made up of the love between us and the new life growing inside me.

With eager anticipation, we began planning for our little bundle of joy, already dreaming of all the memories we would make as a family. Every decision was now centered on her arrival into our lives, and it only added to the excitement building within us.

Some women have a radiant glow when they are pregnant. Not me. From the very moment I found out, I was hit with an unrelenting sickness. It wasn't just the typical morning sickness—it followed me throughout the day and even into the night, making it nearly impossible to get any rest. And then there was the dreaded car sickness—every bump and turn causing waves of nausea to wash over me. I had heard that women experience some degree of sickness during pregnancy, but I couldn't help wondering whether this was normal for all expecting mothers.

I went to the hospital many times during my pregnancy with nausea so severe that I couldn't keep anything down, and I was constantly dizzy. Jeff was incredible and always helping me—so much for the dating phase. I went to the doctor continually with the same complaints as before: earache, hearing loss, ringing in my ear, sinus pressure, headaches, dizziness, and now with the added all-day sickness. I was miserable.

The doctor seemed dismissive, as if pregnancy was the cause of everything in my body. I was floored. How could that be? It seemed like no one believed me when I said I didn't feel normal. A hot flush of emotion washed over me as I realized the full weight of my situation—pregnant, sick, and dismissed.

Somehow, even with all the sickness and chaos, Jeff and I fell even more in love, and we couldn't wait to get married.

As we exchanged vows in front of our fireplace on New Year's Eve surrounded by our closest friends, my swollen belly made it difficult for me to stand for too long. But at that moment, I didn't care about the discomfort or the pregnancy hormones making me emotional and sweaty. It was perfect. As we said, "I do" and sealed it with a kiss, I felt blessed for how much support surrounded us on that special day. We were husband and wife; I couldn't wait to see what other adventures life had in store for us.

Life was definitely about to happen.

2014: The Unexpected When Expecting

In the last few weeks of my pregnancy, I was the sickest I had ever been and experienced the worst headaches. I had to turn the lights down in every room because of the pain it would cause behind my eyes. Even walking from room to room had a chance of making me sick. Many times, I didn't make it to the bathroom before the vomit was out of my mouth. I felt completely out of control of my body.

On February 13, 2014, feeling 90 months pregnant and 90 pounds heavier, I finally went into labor. Jeff made the 45-minute drive to get to the hospital of my choice while I breathed through the painful excitement of minor contractions. Soon after we arrived at the hospital, the contractions and dilation increased, and I was given the option of an epidural. There is a special place in my heart for moms who champion natural birth. For me that's where optimism ends. I had zero interest in rallying for that game. I said, "Yes! Fuck . . . yes, give me the epidural PLEASE!"

Shortly after the injection started numbing the pain, my body found a new way to show its discomfort. My contractions increased and were accompanied by dizzy spells and immediate vomiting. After one of the first episodes of this developing nightmare, I looked up at Jeff, who was holding a bowl under my chin as I was wiping off my still-wet-from-vomit mouth, and said, "You have got to be kidding me." It felt almost cruel that this was going to be a marathon of sickness to seal the deal of having this baby.

The nurses seemed to think it was fine, and while they were very attentive and caring, I was just another pregnant mom they had to care for and get through delivery. My mom, however, who is also a nurse, did not think it was normal. As she sat there holding my hand, careful not to squeeze the IV, she looked at me with concern in her eyes and said, "I never ever experienced anything like this."

I had zero control over my body, my head was spinning, and in that moment her motherly and very justified concern felt more like a bother than something I should pay attention to.

The moment had finally come for the arrival of our precious baby. Jeff stood by one side with a nurse on the other, both providing support with one hand behind my back and the other as a stress toy to calm my shaking hands. My body trembled uncontrollably as I awaited the doctor's command. "One, two, three, PUSH!" The intensity of each push was overwhelming, causing me to spit up more and struggle to catch my breath. The doctor continued to coach me through each contraction, urging me to maintain the strength to push by concentrating on my breathing. The only thing I could concentrate on was getting through this!

Then our beautiful Ava entered the world, and I was overcome with exhaustion and emotion. Sweat caked my face and hair, while vomit lingered around my mouth. With Jeff and the nurse's help, I was finally able to hold our tiny miracle in my arms. She took my breath away with her delicate features and perfect little fingers and toes. In that moment, gazing at her in awe, I experienced a love like no other—instant and unconditional.

Over the course of the year, I was figuring out how to be a mom, remain focused on my career, and enjoy the honeymoon stage with my husband. Meanwhile, all my symptoms persisted, and I was still being treated with a variety of antibiotics, prescriptions, lifestyle changes recommendations, allergy medication, antianxiety medication, and Z-Paks. At one point I told my doctor that there had to be something wrong with my ear since I had so many infections. Her reply was that I might need an adult ear tube. "You do seem to have pain in your ear frequently," she told me. "But let's hold off on the tube for now and try and see if the pain continues before we go that route."

It felt like my doctors' appointments were endless cycles of the same conversation and not anything actionable besides more medicine.

That first year with Ava I was a mess. All new moms are, right? I would sit in her nursery, and she would do tummy time while I would stare off into space. My head constantly felt as if I had just gotten off a boat, and my ear felt full in a way I didn't know how to describe to the doctors anymore. I felt lost.

When Ava was three months old, she was asleep in her crib. I had her windows open, and the late afternoon spring breeze filled the room. I was sitting in the rocking chair my mom had gifted us, and I felt completely numb. Since Ava's birth, I had been to the doctor for my symptoms at least twice a month. The discussion now wasn't only about allergies, sinus infections, and earaches. It was about being tired from work and being a new mom. That was the general explanation for my symptoms. I looked around and saw other new moms who didn't seem to feel like this. *What was wrong with me?*

As I sat there in the rocking chair, my cell phone rang. It was my cousin Amanda. She is as close as I have to a twin sister without having one. I believe in the whole twin connection phenomenon, and we have it. I answered with a low tone, which is not common for my perky personality. "What in the world is wrong with you?" she immediately asked in her normal bossy tone. I told her that I had been sitting in the rocking chair for almost an hour. I felt out of body, my head was wavy, and the thought occurred to me to climb out the open window—no, jump out. Amanda, in very quick, commanding words, told me to call my doctor. She said she was concerned that I may have undiagnosed or delayed postpartum depression.

After about 10 minutes of conversation, I assured her I was not actually going to jump out the window and didn't believe I had postpartum depression. I did agree to stay on the phone with her until Jeff got home. We talked about the big wedding celebration that Jeff and I were going to have in just a few weeks. Yes, we'd had our New Year's Eve wedding ceremony, and we both wanted a big celebration. Selfishly, I wanted to wear a beautiful wedding dress when I wasn't pregnant.

"You know, maybe it is too much to plan another wedding after you just had a baby," Amanda said.

"That's not it," I told her.

"Then help me help you," she pushed. "What are you feeling?"

I paused and then said, "Do you know that I feel sick or maybe tipsy all the time? I don't know what is wrong with me, Amanda, and I am very aware of people thinking I am a hypochondriac if I talk about it too much. I feel crazy sometimes."

Amanda and I grew up in the same family and she empathized with the fear I was voicing. We both had moms we loved and adored, who also worried to the point of being afraid for us to walk outside and look directly at the sun.

"Maybe I am just becoming my mom," I admitted.

Her reply was slow. "Maybe. But I still think you should see your OB-GYN or primary care doctor and tell her all the symptoms. Again."

I appreciated her thoughts and her conversation even more. It did make me feel better, but she didn't know how many times I had shared how I felt. Granted, this felt even lower than before. It had also become my ongoing reality. I was not only questioning myself. Now I felt powerless.

Jeff and I had our second wedding and big, beautiful celebration later that month in Kansas City's Loose Park Rose Garden. It was one of the happiest nights of my life. The excitement of that year and our growing infant helped to overshadow many of my dark days, though it couldn't take them away completely. I continued to push myself to smile even when I didn't want to, and I told myself that if there was really something wrong, the doctors would have found it by now.

2015: Second Time's a Charm

In early 2015, just 18 months after Ava was born, we learned that we were expecting baby number two!

I stumbled out of the bathroom with shaking hands and showed Jeff the pregnancy test. He was thrilled and gave me a tight squeeze! I smiled at him while fighting back the tears. Sure, I was happy about the baby, but I was quietly dreading being pregnant again. In fact, I was terrified. The dizziness, headaches, nausea, and other symptoms had been amplified during the first pregnancy. My body felt completely out of control. I smiled at Jeff, while inside I was thinking, *Oh, no.*

In the weeks to follow, I tried to give myself pep talks as I hovered daily over the toilet. *I am lucky to be pregnant again. I am blessed. This feeling will pass. This is normal.*

If this was normal, then why did my body feel so wrong?

I felt so self-conscious about being seen as a complainer that I stopped talking about all my other symptoms altogether during pregnancy. Through my first pregnancy I remember someone telling me, "You aren't the first woman in the world to be pregnant, so I promise you that you can do this."

During my second pregnancy I forced myself to grin and bear it. To toughen up. To keep the questions, pain, and concern locked inside. Even if the symptoms were poking me to pay attention, I wasn't going to be the overdramatic pregnant woman. No, not me. I was strong.

I felt I wasn't supposed to talk about how awful I was feeling or that it didn't feel normal. The message from everyone around me was clear: just enjoy the blessing of pregnancy.

I vomited nearly every day. This pregnancy was worse than the last. Getting ready for work one morning, I felt so dizzy that I could barely walk. I went to the bathroom and threw up multiple times. I slid down the wall to the floor and felt seasick. Jeff walked into the bathroom, and we decided to go to the ER because I was so weak.

Jeff reached down to help me up. "Come on, honey, it will be okay."

I stood up and flung my arms around him and started sobbing. "What is wrong with me?" I choked out between tears.

"You'll be fine," he said. "Let's go."

When I discussed my symptoms with the ER physician, I told him this pregnancy was worse than the last, and that some of my ever-present symptoms were more extreme than usual. I also shared that my pregnancy had been twins until several weeks ago when I found out the twin had vanished. This is called vanishing twin syndrome when a twin disappears in the uterus because of miscarriage and the fetal tissue gets absorbed by the other twin. Since I had heard hormone levels increased with twins, I suggested that maybe the sickness was a result of the hormones.

As I talked, the physician stared at his computer, entering information. "Maybe," he responded when I paused, not looking at me. He didn't seem particularly interested in what I was saying, and his nonverbal cues confirmed that what I was sharing was normal. I just needed to deal with it.

They gave me a few bags of fluid, monitored me for a while, and sent me on my way, reminding me to drink plenty of liquids, eat frequently, and avoid doing things that made me feel more sick. "Of course." I smiled. "Thank you."

I was exhausted. Yes, I kept smiling, but really I was gritting my teeth, forcing a half-pleasant desperate grin. I didn't feel happy or content. All it seemed I could do was push forward.

I was raging inside. Sure, I will keep drinking my gallons of water, eating saltines until I throw them up too, and basically avoiding everything because everything made me feel dizzy and sick!

Everything in my body was screaming as I got in the car and leaned my head against the passenger window.

Early Christmas morning of 2015, I went into labor. It wasn't easy. Again, I was sick and dizzy 10 times over. I was offered an epidural and gladly took it. This time they administered it incorrectly and only the right side of my body was numb. I couldn't move anything from the waist down on that side. Jeff had to hold my leg up for me to move evenly when they asked. So there I was with my right side completely numb, my left side feeling every second of labor, and the lovely bowl of vomit right beside me.

However, when Jonah, our little Christmas miracle, was born, I was overjoyed. I remember the nurses turning down the lights and handing him to me. As he cried, I started singing "Silent Night," which I had sung while pregnant with him. He stopped crying and stared at me. There is nothing in the world as magical as that first moment you connect with your child. I was exhausted, my head was pounding, I was dizzy, my right side was numb, and still that moment was beautiful.

My first night in the hospital, I woke up each time the nurse brought Jonah to breastfeed. Around four in the morning, I had almost fallen asleep when I felt a rocking motion in my mind and body—the familiar dizzy, seasick feeling, but this time with a subtle hint of something more.

"It feels like there are waves in my head," I told the nurse.

"Well, you just had a baby," she explained. "Your body has been through so much. I am certain you just need to sleep, but please let me know if it continues."

With that, she left the room, and I was left with waves in my head.

I closed my eyes tight and prayed that the voice inside would stop telling me something was very wrong. I just wanted it to go away.

Audacious Optimism in Action

As my story continues, I find myself entering uncharted territory. It's a space that I will wander in for years to come, filled with fear and uncertainty, and feeling dismissed and misunderstood.

Life is a complicated journey, full of unexpected twists and turns. When we feel lost or misunderstood, it's important to remember that everyone has their own unique path. Whether we're starting a new chapter, experiencing job loss, navigating relationships, or searching for answers like I was, it's crucial to trust our inner compass—and fight for bold hope. Oftentimes, the most significant progress is made during trying times, even if we can't see it in the moment. Embrace challenges with a sense of wonder and use discomfort and confusion as motivation to push ahead.

Tips on how to choose audacious optimism during times of uncertainty:

- **Own your individual journey:** Don't allow fear, uncertainty, shame, or comparison with others to diminish your gratitude for your own unique journey. You are one of a kind, and so is the path you're on! A great way to embrace this is by refraining from unnecessary apologies. Only apologize at times such as when you've truly hurt or disrespected someone, but don't apologize for deviating from societal norms, voicing your thoughts, fighting to find the truth, putting boundaries in place, or making choices that align with who you truly are. Take ownership of your journey unapologetically!

- **Acknowledge bias and address it:** Bias is a pervasive force that can even find its way into our own minds. It hides in every corner, slyly influencing our thoughts and actions. But when we become aware of its presence—whether it's in ourselves or others—we have the power to combat it. The next time you're faced with a decision, take a moment to pause and ask yourself, "What assumptions am I making?" Be curious and challenge your thought process and others. And in your daily interactions with others, practice listening without judgment. Take the time to understand their experiences and perspectives before responding. By acknowledging and addressing bias, we can live our best lives and show respect for ourselves and those around us!

- **Curiosity builds courage:** Maintaining a sense of curiosity is essential. Give yourself space to question opinions, relationships, advice, and expertise. Doubt can actually be a positive force when it encourages critical thinking and leads to new insights and perspectives. Make a habit of challenging your assumptions and beliefs every day. Don't simply accept things as they are; instead, ask why they are the way they are. Embrace questioning the status quo and even your own beliefs in order to foster curiosity. Nurturing your curiosity will give you the courage to take risks and help guide you through unfamiliar territory with confidence.

- **Listen to discomfort and confusion:** Instead of viewing emotions such as fear, anger, and sadness as hindrances, recognize them as important messengers from within. They are your inner voice and natural warnings. Rather than suppressing or dismissing them, take a moment to listen to their subtle whispers—that gut feeling. When these feelings arise, pause and close your eyes to acknowledge them. What message do they hold for you? How can knowing they are there help you? By paying attention to these emotions, you may gain valuable insights and be guided toward personal growth and necessary changes.

- **Optimism is not toxic positivity:** Practicing optimism requires conscious determination and effort. It's more than just wishing for the best; it involves actively taking steps toward the best possible outcome. This includes problem-solving, being resilient, searching for the solution, and, regardless of setbacks, holding onto hope for a better future. However, toxic positivity is shallow and disregards reality. It involves denying the truth, suppressing emotions, and having unrealistic expectations. It is not an active approach; instead, it simply hides problems and presents a facade that everything is fine.

Bold hope is not a passive response; it doesn't ignore problems and pretend everything is perfect. Instead, it's a mindful decision to see the good in a situation, even when faced with challenges. It takes effort, determination, and edge. During uncertain times, it is crucial to tighten the straps of your backpack of resilience and sharpen your focus on audacious optimism.

Note

1. Bever, L. (December 13, 2022). "Women's Pain Often Is Dismissed by Doctors." *Washington Post.* https://www.washingtonpost.com/wellness/interactive/2022/women-pain-gender-bias-doctors.

Voice Silenced

Two weeks after having Jonah, I was at home and adjusting to two kids under two years old. It was the first week of January 2016 when I started to see lightning flashes on the side of my right eye. The first few times it happened I jumped, thinking that someone was in my room, or something had moved. Then it registered—it was probably just an eye floater. I get these all the time. The pesky eyelash or something small that makes its way to the back of my eye and floats there for a few minutes, obscuring my vision. That had to be the explanation. However, I went ahead and reached out to the doctor and scheduled an appointment.

After explaining my new symptom, the doctor examined my eyes. She asked me whether any other symptoms were still occurring and then told me she thought I might be experiencing some odd side effects while healing from childbirth. It could even be related to my wrongly administered epidural. She told me to check back after a few weeks if it kept happening.

She moved on and started asking me about everyday life. "How are your anxiety levels?" she asked. In that moment they were high. My brain continued to run without any of the words coming out of my mouth. *Of course there is no other answer. I am so frustrated.*

I left that appointment and just sat in my car for a few minutes, closing my eyes, breathing, and giving myself yet another silent pep talk. *You are not crazy. You are not a hypochondriac. You just need to calm down. You are okay.*

As I opened my eyes, my cell phone started ringing loudly. It was my friend Laura, who always seemed to have impeccable timing with her jokes. A small smile tugged at the corners of my lips as I answered the call. Her first words were a hilarious joke that immediately broke through the tension and made me burst out laughing. Ah, this is exactly what I needed—some humor to mask the real emotions swirling inside me.

As I turned on the car to pull out of the parking lot, she told me I sounded like something was wrong. I explained that I had just left the doctor's office. She let out a knowing sigh and said, "Of course you are." Her words rang true, and I couldn't help laughing, not because it was funny, but rather it was concerning. As I drove away, a sense of unease settled over me. *Maybe I was a hypochondriac. What is happening to me?*

2016: As the World Turns

On January 4, 2016, just 10 days after Jonah was born, another new and terrifying symptom popped up. Jeff and I were in bed and sound asleep. I woke up suddenly feeling as if the room was spinning and I was about to be flung out of bed. I grabbed onto Jeff's arm and screamed as loud as I could. It felt completely real. These weren't the waves I had gotten used to feeling; it was as if the world was spinning. The episode ended after several seconds, and I immediately wobbled to the bathroom and threw up. That was my first experience with extreme vertigo—a sensation of whirling and loss of balance, associated particularly with looking down or caused by disease affecting the inner ear or the vestibular nerve.

I called my doctor as soon as I could and begged for an appointment that day. The nursing team got me right in, and I scrambled to get ready for the appointment. As I drove to the clinic, I was shaking from feeling something so foreign and jarring. I kept telling myself there had to be an explanation. There just had to be one this time.

I walked into the office, and they checked me into one of the clinic rooms. I sat on the exam table and took a few deep breaths. Of course, at that moment I felt fine. No sign of any spinning or vertigo, but it was there somewhere. Hiding in my body. It had been there.

The doctor walked in and saw how upset I was. She seemed concerned and said, "Hey there, I hear you are feeling really bad. What is going on?"

I told her exactly what happened and that it felt as if I was going to get thrown out of bed. "I don't know how else to say this, but I honestly didn't know where the ground was. It felt like the world tipped upside down again and again and again."

"Interesting. I have a hunch what might be causing the vertigo episode," she said, and a flood of relief washed over my body. *Thank God*, I thought. *An answer!*

She had me lie flat on the exam table, grabbed my right arm, placed her other hand behind my upper back, and pushed me to a sitting position as fast as she could.

"Did you feel anything?" she asked.

"No."

She did a few other tests like this. Some with me lying on my back and some on my side. Nothing. She was trying to determine whether I had benign paroxysmal positional vertigo (BPPV), where certain head movements trigger the episodes.

Although tests were inconclusive, she still suspected it to be BPPV. She wanted to explore this more. "There's still a possibility this could be from the aftermath of childbirth, an epidural mistake, maybe even dehydration."

I could feel the prickly claws of panic and anger rising in my body as I began to realize I was about to leave without an answer. Again. For what felt like the thousandth time. She seemed to be doing everything possible to find one. Still no answer. Just more "maybes" and "could be."

As we continued our conversation, she looked through notes on her computer. She also wanted to explore the idea of Ménière's disease. With both the possibilities of BPPV and Ménière's in mind, she referred me to an ear, nose, and throat (ENT) specialist.

Through my patient portal, I could access doctor's notes for each of my many visits to the campus clinic. Sometimes I would log in and look at them to validate that I wasn't crazy. I wanted proof that what was happening wasn't all in my imagination.

For that appointment in January, the assessment notes read: *I think this is BPPV. She had vertigo also when standing for an orthostatics exam* [which can be caused by dehydration], *but BP* [blood pressure] *did not drop. I did not do Epley's* [maneuver used for BPPV treatment to help adjust the crystals in the inner ear] *on her today since her vertigo is severe when it occurs. Discussed ways to make sure she stays on her left side, and she will update me whether she continues to have vertigo.*

The next week, I went to the ENT appointment. Once I checked in, I went back to the exam room to wait for the doctor. It was small and drab brown, and I found myself wishing medical offices were more like day spas—welcoming and therapeutic. Most of them smelled sterile and featured uninviting decor or no decor at all.

I sat there staring at the brown wall for what felt like an hour. As soon as the doctor walked in, he apologized for being behind schedule. I immediately said, "It is okay, I can just jump in and tell you why I am here."

He cleared his throat, took a seat, and said, "Sure."

It was evident that I was impatient from my wait—and this entire journey—and, to his credit, he seemed to understand. I dove right in and went through my entire health history over the last few years, including my current symptoms: headaches, multiple vertigo attacks, seeing a flashing light on my right side, minor hearing problems in my right ear (not yet proven by a hearing test), ringing and fullness in my ear, and general waviness in my head.

He listened intently to me and agreed that my health history and chief complaints seemed to fit with BPPV or Ménière's disease. He told me that Ménière's is an inner ear disorder that causes episodes of vertigo. It usually starts in one ear but may later involve both. Some things can worsen the disease such as smoking, infections, or a high-salt diet.

Well, I do love salt on everything, but the rest is a no, I thought.

The doctor went on to say, "The good news is that both Ménière's and BPPV are treatable."

Finally! I thought. There was a name for something my symptoms could be connected to, and it wasn't rare or life-threatening. While I had lamented the dull exam room just moments ago, my experience with the ENT doctor was a window with just a little light. *Just tell me I have something so I can go fix it.* No matter how scary a diagnosis may be, this is what every desperate patient wants, and I felt that I was finally getting closer to an answer.

I was given a hearing test that showed I had some mild loss of hearing in the right ear. Not many people feel excited to learn that they do, in fact, have hearing loss. I was! It was validation! However, the other test, known as an electrocochleography and used to test how the inner ear muscles react to sound, turned out just fine. My results were consistent with someone who did not have Ménière's. My inner ear muscles were working exactly how they should be, there was no fluid buildup, and I seemed to have a healthy ear.

He didn't think we needed to do any further testing for Ménière's. We talked more about BPPV and the hearing loss in my right ear.

I shared with him that I had been a Kansas City Chiefs cheerleader for nearly a decade in an incredibly loud stadium. "I was once told that this may have caused some problems with my hearing. Do you think this could be the reason my hearing is damaged?"

"I wouldn't be surprised if that's where this mild hearing loss started—cheering in a stadium with that type of sound level for so many years."

I didn't want a co-speculator. I wanted a reason for *why*. Why was this happening? I wanted an answer even if that came in the form of him agreeing with me.

The ENT doctor got up from his stool and leaned against the counter behind him. "Have you discussed with your PCP if there is currently any stress or change in your lifestyle?"

Here we go . . . this again. I sighed and said, "Yes, we talk about it quite a bit. I have two babies, am breastfeeding, back at work, and I am tired. So the symptoms are adding stress to what I would consider normal life."

He smiled and said, "You have your hands full though."

I know he was trying to be kind, but I was annoyed. So freaking annoyed. Yes, I had my hands full, and no, there was not something I could stop doing to relieve stress in my life. I was just living! I was only in my late 30s. There had to be another reason for feeling like I did, other than being a tired working mom.

He told me he could prescribe a common medication, ben-zodiazepines (primarily used to help with anxiety and insomnia), to reduce the symptoms of BPPV, as precaution if I would like. As we discussed this more, he told me that I didn't seem to fit the other markers that would be there with BPPV, but regardless the benzos would help me sleep.

Outwardly, I smiled, as usual. Inside, I screamed. *Sure*, I thought. *Give me medicine to help me sleep, not one to help the world stop spinning*. I declined the medication, mainly because I was breastfeeding. *I don't only need to sleep. I need a damn answer*.

He walked toward the door, and I stood up to shake his hand and wondered why the experts couldn't figure this out.

"Well. thank you," I said. "I wish there were more answers, but at least I know it is nothing serious." The last part I phrased almost as a question back to him. I needed affirmation that it wasn't serious when everything in me kept insisting it was.

"Keep an eye on it and keep your PCP informed if things get worse. Also," he added, sweeping open the exam room door. "Make sure to stay hydrated during your busy day since breast-feeding can really dehydrate your body."

Wow. I had been so hopeful coming into this appointment, and it ended as all the others—without an answer, just a subtle hint that my feelings weren't valid and my symptoms weren't real.

Over the next several weeks, I went back to the doctor many more times. During one of these visits, documented under the assessment and chief complaint on my medical records it read: *She continues to have ongoing problems with intermittent vertigo.*

When I read this note much later in my journey, I felt a rush of emotion over the number of times I had that same conversation about my ongoing vertigo with the doctor. *If I was having ongoing problems, why wasn't something else done? Why were there no other tests outside standard labs run?* There had to be an answer that simply wasn't being found.

Each time I would visit the clinic, the care team provider or doctor would type away at the computer, and I would be able to see everything being documented.

I began to think, *Are your notes really helping you to connect the dots and find answers, or do I just have a really big medical diary?*

Yes, documentation is important in avoiding mistakes caused by human error, such as relying on memory or illegible hand-writing. However, the primary focus on documenting everything hindered the human connection between physician and patient. I was feeling that lack of connection, and I didn't understand it.

Fall 2016: Rinse and Repeat

The year 2016 was a blur for me. I had a two-year-old, an under-one-year-old, and a demanding, exciting, and growing career. I also still had looming health concerns and felt buzzed most of the time.

In August of that year, I had been sick for weeks and needed someone to help me. The doctor treated me for a virus and prescribed Zofran to help control my nausea.

I walked out of the office to the pharmacy to pick up my prescription. I felt deflated. I couldn't help but hear that voice somewhere deep inside of me insisting there was something more. *Go back and ask more questions! Tell them the Zofran can't solve dizziness that won't go away. TELL THEM!*

The pharmacist handed me the pack of pills, and I shakily grabbed them. "Are you okay, Shanna?" she asked.

"No," I told her. "But hoping this helps." I smiled, turned, and walked out to my car.

I sat in the driver's seat and started sobbing. I grabbed the Zofran, popped one from the packet, and quickly put it in my mouth. "WHAT THE FUCK IS WRONG WITH ME?!" I screamed out as I kept crying. My outburst felt like purging for the soul—releasing all the anger and frustration at once. It felt good, and I started to breathe and calm down.

While I was having this episode alone in my car, my doctor was inside and had documented in my medical record: *Suspect this is viral with the achiness. Zofran for nausea. Consulted with pharmacy—okay while breastfeeding. Ibuprofen with some food for achiness. BRAT diet. Push fluids. Update me if not better. Her vertigo has been persistent. I don't think it should be happening still. Will wait until over this acute issue and then may consider brain MRI.*

There is no word to describe the haunting feeling I have when I think back to that comment. I often wonder how less conservative care would have changed my story.

Even after that viral infection passed, I was in a constant fog. The waves in my head continued their daily tide of pressure in and out—compression, then decompression. At times, it was barely noticeable; at others, it would physically knock me off my feet.

It was obvious by this time in my health care journey, I knew in the depth of my soul that I wasn't getting the answers I needed. However, this started an equally weighted battle between advocacy and self-doubt. I didn't have anyone else at these appointments advocating for and with me. It was just me. It had just been me for years, and the sound of my own voice was becoming less frequent and more muted, so I wasn't even my own trusted advocate. When I did speak up and ask a question, I felt crazy. Even the way I voiced my concerns began to sound passive. My self-doubt was in the driver's seat. I needed the advocate in me—the me who knew better—but somewhere along the road of all these appointments, lack of answers, and no other tests, she'd lost her way.

Winter 2016: You're Fine

I had just walked back from my office after seeing my kids at the day care located on the corporate campus. I sat down, took off my big winter coat, and looked blankly at my computer screen. I not only felt waves in my head, but I could see them in the words weaving up and down on the screen. The area behind my right eye and side of my head throbbed. My brain fog was so bad that I felt disconnected from reality.

I turned to one of my colleagues and told her what was happening. She told me that I seemed a little spacey and suggested we walk to the clinic and ask for an urgent care appointment. I took her advice and offer, and we made the walk. When we arrived, they got me in right away, and I was able to see my primary care doctor. She had a conversation with me for a few minutes and asked what I had been doing before this spell hit. I told her I went to see the kids and was breastfeeding. She had someone bring me juice, water, and crackers, wondering whether I was suffering from low blood sugar or loss of electrolytes.

As I talked with her, she said that I just didn't seem right. *I KNOW,* I thought. I was typically an energetic, and high-functioning individual. She told me she was a bit concerned by this episode in which the symptoms seemed to present themselves as focal neurological symptoms (automatic movement changes, weakness, loss of muscle control). Out of an abundance of caution, she sent me to the emergency room (ER) at the acute care hospital across the street to make sure nothing was missed.

When I arrived, the ER doctor discussed my symptoms. He told me that we were going to do an exam with cross-sectional imaging, better known as a CT scan, but it may take a bit before it was ready. In the meantime, I lay in the bed, closed my eyes, and took in the bag of fluids they had hooked up to my arm. This made me think of my dad holding onto an IV pole years ago. Although, he had answers, even if it meant there was no cure. He had answers—a diagnosis, even if life-altering, provides a path for acceptance and action.

A few hours later, they walked me to the CT exam room. I immediately got nervous. They had me lie on the CT bed board, and I saw the massive and intimidating arch above where my head would be.

I laid down and they started to put in my IV, explaining that the contrast would be used for one of the images. I was shaking and I said, "Sorry, I just feel so nervous and this has been a really long day." The nurse who was attending to me said, "The more you move, the longer this will take." That is all he said to me. There was zero compassion, zero empathy. Just instruction to stop talking, stop moving so we could get it done. I closed my eyes and lay as still as I could and felt tears roll down my face. I knew their job was tough and they dealt with challenging people sometimes, but at that moment, I didn't feel like a person at all.

They ran the CT twice. Once without contrast and once with. It was quick and painless. I was back in my ER room where I found Jeff waiting for me. Delighted to see him, I gave a weak smile and hugged him.

He gave me a huge hug and grabbed my hand. "We will figure out why you are feeling like this all the time," he assured me. "I will be here for you, I'll do bedtime with the kids, and we can have a competition drinking water and only make healthy food. We got this, Babe."

He pointed to the sign on the hospital wall with the pain number scale from 1 to 10. Underneath each number was a face. One was happy and 10 was extremely sad. The hospital clinicians use this tool for kids to help them describe their pain level. "So, where are we at now on this chart?" Jeff asked.

I gave him my most pathetic pouty face with tears in my eyes and said, "A ten." We both laughed, mine combined with some crying, but it still felt good.

While I loved his support, and of all people, I was on board with his positive attitude, I didn't tell him that there was more to this and I didn't know what it was. Every test showed that I was fine, but my insides were still screaming and my world was still spinning. I needed an answer. I needed something to act on. I wanted the doctor to come back and say, "We have an answer, and this is how we'll solve it." I didn't tell Jeff any of this because I had lost so much trust in myself that I felt embarrassed to continue to share how I felt. I just let him wipe my laughing tears away and kiss my forehead.

I squeezed my eyes shut tight. There would be an answer—a way forward. I prayed for the doctor to walk through the door, validate my concerns, and declare a solution. A glimmer of hope ignited in my core, urging me to cling to the belief that today would be the day, the first step toward recovery.

The ER doctor came in a little while later with the report and gave me a quick smile before looking at the folder of papers in his hand. "Your brain looks great on the CT scan, and we didn't see anything of concern."

My heart sank. As much as I wanted there to be nothing catastrophically wrong, I wanted something conclusive. That is the funny thing about searching for answers. You want to find something, but you don't want to find something, but you need to find something to do something about it.

No. No. No! I felt defeated.

The doctor then talked about my lifestyle, how tired I was, and maybe checking in with my eye doctor to see whether there was something going on with my vision that could be causing these spells.

I just sat there and let him talk. I wanted to tell him I'd already seen my eye doctor and my eyes were fine. I wanted to say that if he sent me back, my eye doctor would probably just refer me to another specialist. I was on a fucking hamster wheel and I had no clue how to get off. No one believed me, every test came out fine, and maybe I was just an exhausted, mildly crazy working mom. All of this stayed in my head, and I started to zone out until he made his next comment.

"You may just be a really tired and overworked mom."

I gave him a blank stare and started to quiver as if I were cold, but I wasn't cold. My body was having a physical reaction to his dismissive words. Jeff squeezed my hand because he knew. He knew I felt that comment like a dagger to my very soul.

"You should try and take some time off from work if you can," the doctor advised.

I felt small. I felt demoralized. I felt embarrassed. I felt so much self-doubt that I wanted to curl up in a ball and rock myself to sleep.

Ever since my father passed away when I was nine years old, in my saddest moments I feel the pain of that loss again. It is like a wound that will never heal that only surfaces when something has truly broken me open.

That was this moment—sitting in what might have been my 70th, 80th, or 90th appointment in five years, being told, again, there was nothing wrong.

Instead, I said nothing. Nothing at all, and they sent me home.

I later read my ER discharge record. They documented the chief complaint as the following: *36 y/o F who presents for head, dizziness. She notes since January has had dizziness, which has been evaluated by both her PCP and an ENT. ENT suggest tx* [treatment] *for BPPV* [benign positional vertigo] *however she deferred medication due to nursing. She notes she went to PCP today for evaluation of throbbing headache she has had behind her R* [right] *eye, along with nausea. She states also has pain along the R side of her scalp. She notes flashes of lights that have occurred with pain.*

The CT reading showed my brain as being normal for my age with no excessive atrophy, mass, hemorrhage, or abnormal enhancements. I would later find out from the surgeons who performed my life-saving procedure that according to their review of the actual CT film, the radiology team missed the severe misalignment of my brain stem. Had this been identified, it would have saved me one year of brain tumor growth. A person missed this. Maybe they looked away, were new to reading the scan, or maybe they were tired. This was human error, not the machine. If I would have spoken up in the ER, thrown a tantrum and demanded another review or a second reading of the CT scan—if I would have questioned the response they gave me—if I would have chosen to listen to my instinct and done something, it may have saved me one year.

Twelve months of time lost with my family while feeling the fatigue of a disease no one knew was there.

That's 365 days of feeling stuck on a hamster wheel not able to find a way off.

Or 8760 hours of an imposter in my body stealing my choice, my voice, my self-trust, my confidence, my determination, my time, my life.

The moment the doctor told me my CT report was fine, it wiped away all my self-belief. It was at that moment I told myself, *Enough. Calm down, Shanna. You're fine. Stop trying to find something wrong when there's nothing.*

I had been searching in the darkness for too long, trying to find the way forward. It felt as if there was no one there with me. No one felt my pain. No one believed me. No one knew I was in this darkness alone.

When they didn't see something wrong with my brain, I took it as the final answer. The last straw. The crushing blow.

For the past five years, I had been down the long road of misdiagnosis, antibiotics, antianxiety meds, blood tests, and specialist appointments searching for something that was not there. I had been told time and time again there was nothing wrong and I needed to listen.

So I did.

I was fine.

I was fine.

But I wasn't fine, and my inner voice knew it. Deep down that faint whisper was being suffocated—lost in the darkness with no light.

When I went back to see my doctor, she came in and confirmed again that the CT was clear. She asked me how I felt, and

I told her that I "guessed" I was fine. She then went on to say, "We could go ahead and do an MRI if you would like, just to have one more confirmation that we aren't missing anything." I half-heartedly agreed.

The imaging office called about a week later to schedule the scan, and I never called back. The message came and went, and I didn't schedule an appointment. It was clear to me my doctor thought this test was unnecessary.

It is disheartening and maddening to know that patients get so far down the road of unexplained symptoms that they doubt themselves. This is exactly what happened to me. Enough people, enough experts, told me I was fine. I had to believe them, which meant giving up.

I didn't call back. The appointment was never scheduled. Nobody located the brain tumor that had been missed on the CT scan. My doctor's office didn't follow up to question why I hadn't followed through. So the tumor grew.

I was underinformed and thought that if a CT scan didn't detect any problems with my brain, then an MRI wouldn't either. However, about 4% of brain tumors are missed each year with a CT scan, according to a 2022 study published in *Canadian Association of Radiologists Journal* (Lu and Lysack 2022).[1] This happens due to human error, fatigue, and distractions, or simply being unable to spot a small tumor.

Mine wasn't small. It was the size of a golf ball. A golf ball lodged behind my right ear—a golf ball that was growing bigger by the day.

On December 12, 2016, I returned to the doctor with the same foggy symptoms in addition to pressure behind my right eye, headaches, dizziness, and tenderness on the right side of my face and head.

I was treated for sinusitis and given another Z-Pak with instructions to rest and drink fluids.

I stopped trusting my body, my heart, and myself. I lost my voice and my fight.

Audacious Optimism in Action

Life can often feel like a relentless cycle of chaos and confusion, an unending whirlwind that leaves you feeling lost and uncertain. It feels as if you are constantly chasing after something that may seem elusive, whether it be an answer to health problems, or the perfect career or relationship, or simply trying to find your place in the world. These feelings can arise at any point in your life, as I am sure they have already, from the turbulence of youth to the uncertainties of adulthood. During moments of change and challenge, it's easy to feel overwhelmed and directionless.

In these times, it's important to stay true to yourself and remember you have a choice—you always have a voice. Cling onto hope and faith for a brighter future full of new opportunities, even when you feel stuck, alone, or misunderstood. It's during these trials that resilience is truly tested and refines you into a stronger individual.

Tips on how to choose audacious optimism during times of confusion:

- **Master the art of advocating:** People crave answers—don't give up until you find them. Question yourself: What do I stand for? What do I believe in? What do I know needs to change? If you're seeking solutions for yourself, don't accept anything less than what satisfies you. And if you're advocating for someone else, don't settle on their behalf. Ambiguity doesn't benefit anyone. Take actual notes, not just mental notes. Keep persevering. Keep pushing. Keep posing inquiries. Challenge yourself to persist and continue asking questions and stand up for what you believe.

- **Gratitude, gratitude, gratitude:** Even when life hands you rotten lemons, there is always something to be thankful for. Sometimes the challenges may seem too difficult to handle, or you have endured them for too long. For these moments, every morning try to find at least one thing that makes you feel grateful or brings a smile to your face. And if there's nothing in your immediate surroundings, seek out inspiration from others who practice gratitude. Find uplifting stories, motivational quotes, and role models. Read biographies of people who have overcome adversity, watch inspiring videos, or follow *positive* social media accounts (note my emphasis on positive). Let their experiences serve as your motivation to express gratitude.

- **Feel your feelings, even anger:** Just like the popular movie *Inside Out*, our emotions are intricate and varied. Even seemingly negative ones, such as anger, serve a purpose. Rather than pushing them aside or suppressing them, we should see them as a valuable tool trying to convey something important. When anger arises within me, whether due to work, my children, or just daily frustrations, I often pause whatever I'm doing and step away for a moment, then I count to 10. This forces me to give myself time to process the emotion without reacting impulsively. On a deeper level, anger may indicate feeling misunderstood, experiencing an injustice, having our boundaries violated, or having unmet needs. It's crucial to acknowledge our emotions so we can address the underlying causes instead of simply reacting in a heated manner or ignoring them entirely.

- **Celebrate progress:** Celebrate every step, no matter how small, that you take forward. Whether it's conquering a difficult obstacle or finding the strength to maintain a hopeful mindset for just one more day, give yourself credit for your progress. Be kind to yourself and recognize the effort you have put in. Through my health journey, there were times when my only celebration was just making it through another day, but it was a victory worth acknowledging. Celebrating yourself is an act of self-care—like taking a moment to look at your reflection in the mirror and smile at the person staring back at you.

- **Learn from setbacks and failure:** Challenges are a natural and unavoidable part of life, and when faced with them, setbacks and failures are bound to happen. However, these should not be seen as defeats or barriers to progress. Instead, use them as opportunities for growth and improvement. When faced with setbacks or failures, take a moment to reflect on what went wrong and where there may be gaps in your understanding. Then adjust or change your approach accordingly and try again. Keep pushing forward, no matter how many times you have to go through this cycle. Each time you do so, your resilience grows stronger.

Audacious optimism, at times, is gritty and fuels resilience and the courage to keep moving forward, even when life feels like a repetitive cycle. The cycle will end!

Note

1. Lu, F., & Lysack, J. T. (2022). Lessons learned from commonly missed head and neck cancers on Cross-Sectional Imaging. *Canadian Association of Radiologists Journal*, 73(3), 595–597. https://doi.org/10.1177/08465371221079107

Without a Spark

New Year's Eve, 2016: Vodka Salad

My team at work had planned an epic New Year's Eve party as a fundraiser (called EVE), and I couldn't wait to revel in the festivities as a guest, not a speaker. The perfect company of Jeff and my sister and brother-in-law, Melissa and Jamie, only added to the excitement—their infectious energy and Jamie's inappropriate jokes always guaranteed a good time. Let's not forget about the vodka cocktails that seemed to flow endlessly throughout the night.

Vodka has always been my go-to social indulgence—its low-calorie count being a major selling point for me. In fact, I even have my own signature drink: the Vodka Salad.

Take note, dear reader, because this recipe is a staple:

- *Vodka (your choice—mine is Grey Goose)*
- *soda water and ice*
- *all the fruit from the bar condiment caddy (lemon, lime, cherry, orange, mint, the possibilities are endless)*

With my trusty Vodka Salad in hand and feeling fabulous in my outfit, I boldly declared that 2017 would be an incredible year. I was determined to make this year the best one yet!

When I woke up the morning of January 1, 2017, it was a new year, but the same pounding headache greeted me. My vision was blurred and my legs felt like Jell-O as I stumbled out of bed. The hangover hit me like a tsunami, leaving me nauseated and unable to function properly. But alas, duty called in the form of two rambunctious toddlers who demanded my attention.

However, there was something very different about that terrible hangover.

My headache felt as if someone had hit me with a baseball bat in the back of my head behind my right ear. I could have taken a

Sharpie and drawn exactly where this feeling was. It was so distinct. That part of my head throbbed, and the flashes of light that had started in my right eye a year ago were intense.

Jeff also felt less than 100% yet still managed to take care of me. He got me an ice pack for the side of my head, turned off the lights, and let me sleep.

The hangover passed, as they do, but the feeling stuck with me. I touched the back of my head again right at the base of my skull by my right ear, remembering the strange throbbing that had been there. Almost as if there was swelling only in that part of my head. *That is not possible though, right? I mean, what a weird place for a migraine.*

I sat there for a moment and just kept my hand on that spot, pressing to see whether I felt any pain. Nothing. Just in case it was related to indulging too much, I decided on a dry January and maybe even February.

A few weeks later in the middle of the night, I suffered one of the worst episodes of vertigo since they had begun. It started just like the others. I was sleeping, felt pushed into a spin, woke up, screamed, and grabbed Jeff's arm. This time I couldn't get it to stop. I threw myself out of bed and gripped onto the carpet until it stopped. Then I threw up.

What was happening, and why was this happening?!

I felt so alone in the darkness of my feelings. I needed a spark. I needed something, so I started to write in a journal about the episodes:

"I feel so awful again today."

"What is wrong with me?"

"I feel like I am living just outside of my body most of the time. I need help."

"No one sees it, but I need some sort of help."

I look back at these writings and see that I was depressed, I was scared, and my body was trying so hard to help me crack this case.

Spring 2017: Drink Your V-8

I made another appointment mid-spring of 2017 to tell my doctor that I still felt the waves in my head and the constant dizziness. As I walked into the doctor's office, I heard someone yell, "Shanna!" That brought me to a quick stop.

One of my coworkers gave me a smile and said, "Wow, you are in a daze. You literally walked past me, and I even said your name a few times."

"Oh gosh, I am so sorry." It was not the first time I'd heard this comment. I was missing things—such as people talking to me. "I am a little tired today," I explained before joking, "and it seems there's not enough coffee in the world for me these days!"

We both laughed, and he said, "I absolutely get that."

Maybe I wasn't hearing them, or maybe this dizzy, buzzed state had put me in a complete brain fog. It was weird. I felt it, and others were starting to take notice.

I was sitting on the exam table fiddling with my phone when the doctor walked in.

"Hey there, so I hear you are still feeling dizzy." She sat down across from me and pulled the computer keyboard close to her to start typing, which prompted me to dive in.

I told her everything I was still feeling. The constant dizziness and a new feeling that I was tilted all the time. I said with a laugh of embarrassment, "The best comparison I have for this is the old V-8 commercials, where I am just tilted, and I need something to help me walk straight again."

You may remember the V-8 commercials in the late 80s. A boss arrived at the office walking slanted off the elevator. The admin (who was a woman of course) would ask him what he'd had for breakfast. He would say something very unhealthy, and she would hand him a V-8, a drink claiming to be loaded with vegetables, to help him walk straight. After the boss took a sip, the admin piped in with the tagline, "Drink V-8 and get straight!"

The doctor laughed with me as I shared the V-8 comparison and said, "Wouldn't it be great if things were that easy?"

No, but really, yes. Yes, it would, I thought to myself. I said, "Well, I wake up every morning, make my coffee, drive to work, walk inside the office, and sit down, feeling like my ground zero is slightly slanted. Which sounds crazy coming out of my mouth. Let me try another analogy. Umm . . . I guess it's sort of like the moment when you have that first drink, and you feel that buzz. A tipsy sensation and a fog set in, and you become a little wobbly."

"Hmmm . . ." she pondered as she looked back at my electronic file. "I wonder if you are struggling with some seasonal allergies. I am seeing this a lot right now. With your history of ear and sinus problems this can be brought on or made worse by allergies and impact your balance and cause you to feel dizzy."

Well, that seemed very logical. Maybe allergies were the cause of everything. Everything over the past several years. Maybe allergy medication would be my V-8!

This had to be the answer.

It had to be.

I called my husband on the way home and said, "I have allergies."

"Okay," he responded, sounding confused. "Um, why do you sound happy about it?"

"Because I think this is the cure I have been seeking out. Apparently, allergies can increase as you age, which makes sense that I didn't even know I had them." We talked a bit longer, and for the first time in a long time, I felt a moment of rest with hope; I was going to pop a Zyrtec in my mouth, spray my nostrils with Flonase, and return to feeling like myself again.

Over the course of the next several weeks, I dove into the new allergy remedy routine. It absolutely did help with the allergies I didn't even know I had (e.g., itchy eyes, some sinus pressure). It did not solve the vertigo, dizziness, headaches, hearing loss, or slanted feeling. About three weeks after starting the routine, I realized this was not the fix-all for my symptoms.

I woke up one morning after a night with an intense vertigo episode, and I stood over my bathroom sink staring at myself in the mirror. I tried to smile. I said to tell myself out loud, "You're fine."

I wanted so badly to believe that girl in the mirror saying I was fine. I was beginning to not even recognize her. *Who was she?* All these symptoms had at one time seemed short-lived, bearable episodes. Now, as I stared at my sad appearance in the mirror, I saw myself living the rest of my life with this silent torture. I felt lonely. I felt misunderstood. I felt invisible. No one saw me, heard me, or knew my pain.

How did I end up here? And with no possible answers?

Despite my inner turmoil and lack of answers, I felt the immense pressure to maintain the facade of an energetic and put-together mother, a supportive and loving wife, successful at my job, and a social butterfly. It was the image that I came to believe everyone expected me to uphold, and any sign of weakness or struggle might polarize people's perceptions of me. So, day after day, I wore this mask for others. Only two people saw through it: Jeff and my mom. They witnessed my daily struggles—from almost collapsing under the weight of it all to experiencing bouts of vertigo and foggy thinking as well as uncontrollable mood swings that were a stark contrast to my usual life-loving demeanor.

To the rest of the world, I perfected the illusion that everything was fine. From the outside, I looked like my usual go-getter cheerful self. On the inside, I was crying out for help. I longed for knowledgeable and connected care, where I felt truly understood and my doctors had access to all the necessary information at their fingertips. A world without barriers to data, where they could easily compare me to other patients with similar symptoms—from around the world—and find the answer quickly. Instead, I felt trapped in a disjointed system of appointments that left me feeling lost, misunderstood, and alone in the dark.

Audacious Optimism Action Steps

I'm sure you can recall a moment in your life when you felt as lost as I did during this part of my journey. It's a feeling of being completely adrift, with no sense of understanding for your own circumstance, direction, or purpose. Yet, amid this uncertainty, I found moments to cling to small glimmers of hope in small actions.

I firmly believe that each and every one of us has the capability to face, accomplish, and overcome impossible challenges, even if we are not aware of our own inner strength. Even in the darkest of times, you can continue to move forward, searching for any faint sign of light or guidance. Keep breathing, keep moving, keep searching; the path may be difficult, but you will find your way.

Tips on how to choose audacious optimism when you feel lost:

- **Confront reality:** Life resembles a winding road, with all the twist and turns that frequently thrust unforeseen challenges on us. Frankly speaking, life can throw you a shitstorm. In such moments, mere solutions or quick fixes fall short; instead, they demand a gritty optimism. Simple positivity won't suffice; and in order to choose hope you must first confront reality head-on and then take decisive action on what you will do next. What is in your control and what is out of your control? What steps can you take to either improve the situation or just simply move forward? While accepting harsh truths can be arduous, within those moments lie some of the most extreme growth, progress, and new-found strength—much like scaling a colossal mountain: bold and daring.

- **Set small goals:** While it's important to have big, ambitious goals, it's the smaller, incremental steps that lead you toward desired change. Breaking down larger goals into more manageable pieces not only makes them less daunting but also increases your chances of success. Allow yourself to dream and believe that seemingly impossible goals are within your reach. Write them down. Then, write down the small actions you can take toward that vision—make one call, show up to the meeting, ask to be invited to the meeting, have the conversation that maybe you don't want to have with someone, etc. These goals should push you out of your comfort zone and subconsciously inspire you to do more. The excitement of an audacious goal can fuel motivation and determination, while taking small steps makes them attainable.

- **Practice mindfulness:** When you feel that life is moving on without you, and your small steps just aren't enough, it's natural to feel disconnected and lost. However, it's important to take the time to understand why this is happening. By incorporating mindfulness into your daily routine, you can improve your overall well-being and become more present in every moment. Start your day with intention by setting aside some time before checking your phone or email and just close your eyes and breathe. Throughout the day, practice mindfulness during everyday activities such as brushing your teeth or getting dressed. Pay attention to your senses in these moments.

Of course, if you have the time and the luxury to do it, dedicate specific time each day for formal mindfulness practices such as intentional breathing exercises, yoga, or other self-care techniques.

- **Journal and reflect:** This is actually a great method of mindfulness—journal. Allow yourself a moment of contemplation and use a pen and paper or your phone's Notes app to record your thoughts. Writing is a therapeutic way to work through emotions and connect with your inner being (if you can't tell by how many times I've mentioned it already). It may be beneficial to revisit these entries periodically to monitor your development and evolution. In fact, that's exactly what I did while writing this section of the book! Journaling can often be the only way to express our true selves, and we all require an outlet for thoughts that others may not comprehend, or those that we have yet to fully grasp.

- **Share the load:** It is crucial to find your tribe, your crew, your team, the ones who truly comprehend you and will love and support you—especially during the darkest times. These genuine connections provide a sense of community, empathy, and a safe haven where you can be vulnerable. They also don't have to be the same people for every situation. Just like a work team, the people on your life team come with their own strengths, and love them for that—they might show up at your door when you need them or just with a loving emoji in your text. Either way, they will show up. Lean on these relationships when you feel that you have no more strength left. This could mean simply asking someone to keep you company or sending a message that says, "I'm feeling down; could you send me something positive?" Don't hesitate to reach out for help when needed—your loved ones will show up, and you don't have to bear the weight alone. Whether it's seeking professional assistance or confiding in a friend, allowing someone else to share the burden is courageous.

Keep going—finding hope in the darkest and most challenging moments takes audacity, and you have it!

Let's Recharge

Wow! This point in my health journey feels heavy right now—I feel it too! In writing this, I felt the heaviness all over again. I felt the injustice and the unbelievable logic that no answers meant no problems.

You probably gathered from my earlier life stories that I was always a naturally positive person. I had pep in my step, and my glass was typically half full. I maintained an upbeat attitude and lifted others up when they were feeling low. However, during my health journey, I had to confront the fact that positivity is just a feeling, most likely dependent on circumstances of happiness. Audacious optimism is different—it is a mindful choice; it requires conscious effort and intentionality. It takes deliberate determination to choose optimism and cling to hope and self-assurance while navigating an unknown path.

The seemingly anticlimactic stop on my journey feels like an endless tunnel of darkness, a place I still shudder to remember. It was here that I lost sight of who I truly was, as my trust in myself shattered under the weight of being unheard and undervalued in our health care system.

Everything we experience shapes us into who we are. I didn't realize it at the time, of course, but I was laying the foundation for audacious optimism. I had to be at my lowest to know the steps to climb back up, even higher than before, and understand the active nature of audacious optimism—which begins with a

145

mindful choice, trusting yourself, embracing the unknown, and tapping into mental toughness.

Optimism is not an easy state of mind that aligns with being happy. It is a gritty choice we make in our darkest moments, forcing ourselves to see beyond the darkness and hold onto the belief that the impossible can become possible.

It takes immense strength to choose bold hope over the path of fear, doubt, sadness, and loneliness. We have all been in those dark places, where hope seems impossible to grasp. Throughout my life, I have always marched to the beat of my own drum, trusting my instincts, and not wanting to remain status quo. I've always been ambitious and determined, constantly seeking out new experiences and challenges. I learned to trust my own voice and believe in my abilities and willpower. Rarely did I just blindly follow others, and when I did—sometimes by choice, sometimes out of naivete—it never turned out to be the best decision for me. I learned along my life journey that I was a questioner, a discoverer, an explorer, and a conqueror for whatever life had in store.

However, when faced with this seemingly insurmountable obstacle, my natural positivity was no match for the harsh reality of my situation. Optimism wasn't going to come to me like a breezy feeling. I had to boldly choose it.

Now let's jump into the story back where this book began, fall 2017, the moment I found out that I had a brain tumor.

The Diagnosis

Fall 2017: A Golf Ball

As I hung up the phone with the doctor, his words echoed in my mind. I had a brain tumor: *it is large, rare, and life-threatening.* I could feel every moment that had led up to this one rush over me like roaring waves. The countless times I had complained of dizziness, the moments when sounds faded into nothingness, the intense vertigo that left me feeling helpless. All the symptoms that I couldn't explain but knew were real. Every useless medication prescribed, every misdiagnosis, all the times I had been dismissed as being a hypochondriac, a tired mom, or simply dehydrated. The frustration and pain of seeking answers for five long years. And now here we were, finally facing the truth—my body had been trying to tell me something was wrong all along. And someone finally gave me the space to advocate for myself, listened to me, and didn't stop until they found the answer.

Tears streamed down my face. The years I spent alone with an imposter in my head felt like a suffocating eternity. I wasn't able to reach Jeff, so I called my mother-in-law, Ann. When she arrived at our house she pulled me into her arms. She promised me that everything would be okay. She pulled back and looked at me as she cried too, and we both knew that this was life-changing and wouldn't be easy.

I don't remember if I said anything to her. I just let her keep pulling me into hugs followed by comforting words. I cried and cried and cried. I told her what the doctor had said and what time I had to be back in their office tomorrow. Then I stared blankly into space and asked if she would make dinner for Jeff and the kids. I walked upstairs to my bedroom. I got in bed, pulled the covers over my head, and sobbed.

Ann told Jeff all the details, and, at some point in the night, he lay down beside me and said, "You are the strongest person

149

I know. Whatever this is—you can beat it. I just know you can, and we will all be right there with you."

I lay there internalizing the moment, hoping that if I just closed my eyes long enough, this would all go away. Shock paralyzed me. I wanted to stay under those covers, so I did.

At some point in the morning, I woke up and started to think about the changes in the last 24 hours. This diagnosis was one that I did not choose, but it was also something I had been searching for. It was hard to believe that yesterday seemed so normal and today felt like the aftermath of an explosion. An explosion I felt brewing. I wanted a diagnosis, but not this diagnosis.

I was back again facing that black bear, and this time I couldn't run. I had to face it. I had to stare it down with bold confidence. I had to stand strong.

Jeff and I walked together into the appointment the next day. We weren't only going to see the ENT specialist. We first saw the hospital's department chair of neurosurgery. The minutes Jeff and I waited for him felt like hours. He walked into the exam room with a warm and somber smile. The hair on my arms stood up. *What did he know that I was about to find out?*

After a few nice greetings, he told me that the tumor was an acoustic neuroma. It is considered rare, meaning they only develop in two out of every 100,000 people. This tumor is a noncancerous tumor on the main nerve leading from the inner ear to the brain. It usually grows slowly if it grows. However, in a few cases, it becomes large enough to press against the brain and affect vital functions. This was my case.

He gave us an actual answer to every single one of my symptoms. Every. Single. One. It wasn't a hunch or a guess to solve one or two symptoms. Cases like mine were considered life-threatening because the tumor had outgrown the small canal that connects the inner ear to the brain. It was growing in my skull cavity.

"Typically, this is a tumor that we would just monitor if it were small enough, like the size of a seed or even an almond," the surgeon explained. "If it were even just a little larger than that, we would treat it with a procedure known as the middle fossa approach, which removes the tumor and preserves the hearing. However, that is not possible in your case."

My breath caught in my throat at the realization that this noncancerous tumor had been allowed to grow to a point large enough to be life-threatening—out of the reach of traditional treatment.

"The tumor that we found is approximately 4.5 cm, roughly the size of a golf ball, and considered very large, even giant. It is compressing your brain stem. Your life expectancy from this point based on the size and positioning of the tumor could be as little as one year without surgery to extract some of the mass and relieve the pressure from your brain."

Anger. Disbelief. Shock. Sadness.

I got up from my chair and started pacing. The room was too small. I felt as if I were hovering outside of my body and hearing things through a tunnel. I needed to catch my breath and feel movement, some blood flow in my body. That fight-or-flight feeling was pumping hard through my veins. I wanted to run. I wanted to scream. *This is not my story*, I thought. *This can't be my story!*

I closed my eyes, and I wanted to jump out the window. Jeff squeezed my hands. I pushed back the tears and choked on a few deep breaths.

You cannot run from this, Shanna, I said to myself. I had to be active, I had to participate, I had to face this damn tumor, and I had to believe that I could face it. This is what I had been looking for all those years. A diagnosis. This is what my inner voice had been telling me was there.

The surgeon explained the care plan the team would be discussing. It most likely would be the rectosigmoid approach involving an incision behind the ear and removal of the bone to expose the tumor. Their aim would be to remove a portion of the tumor, maybe less than 50%, just enough to relieve pressure on my brain and make sure they wouldn't damage the nerves that control movement in the face. After the surgery, I would undergo radiation therapy to shrink it even further. While this would be the best method of decreasing the size of the tumor between the first, second, and possibly third surgery, radiation brought a risk of increasing the tumor's size, along with other side effects.

He told me that he had "only" performed the type of surgery I needed on a tumor my size 421 times.

First, that is what I needed to know. I thought to myself, *Only 421 times?*

Is that enough experience?

It doesn't seem like it at all.

I mean, this is my freaking brain and my life.

Well, I guess if there's only two in 100,000 people with this tumor and most are caught way before one of my size, maybe 421 is a lot.

But what are his outcomes?

He is an expert surgeon obviously, but is he the best expert for the tumor I have?

This care plan is going to involve maybe two or more surgeries with radiation—there must be another way.

Second, I was deeply thankful for his kind and thorough explanation of the diagnosis and treatment. As he continued to talk, I started to feel that the proposed care plan was not for me. It felt suffocating because it didn't offer the hope and the future I envisioned for myself. I didn't know whether I could find a plan that did, but I needed to try.

I knew this was the only answer in some scenarios, but I had to be sure it was my only answer before choosing it. If this tumor was in *my* head, I was ready to break down any barrier to get myself the right care. I didn't care how much it cost or how much time I had to spend on it. I'd already spent years finding my diagnosis. I was going to find my treatment plan.

We tentatively scheduled the surgery with the clinical team as well as my future appointments. However, I knew I was going to spend the next few weeks figuring out how to get another opinion and care plan option. I thanked the surgeon and left.

On the car ride home, Jeff and I were silent. He tried to make some jokes, which he always does so well, but he could see my wheels and my emotions spinning.

"I think I need to reach out to people," I told him. "I don't even know if I know what I mean yet, but just sharing what's happening with others. What we just heard in that doctor's office sounded like maybe there's a better option. I don't know how I know it, but I just do, and I need to figure out how to find it."

When we walked through the door of our house, I immediately sat down, grabbed my phone and my computer, and reached out. I sent a message to my colleagues, my close friends, and to Maria Menounos through her website. Then I created a post on Instagram.

It felt surreal to type out the journey of the past five years and where it had led.

I had an overwhelming response from colleagues. A flooding sense of community surrounded me right away, and I knew I wasn't in this alone. I had people ready to cheerlead for the cheerleader. Some shared their personal stories. Others asked me whether I was getting a second opinion and how they could help. Their support was the spark I needed.

When I emailed Maria Menounos through her website, I never considered I might get a response, but I wanted to reach out regardless. There had been so many signs telling me to get off the road of self-doubt, but Maria's story had been the speed bump that slowed me down and made me take a small step to take back the wheel.

To my surprise, just two short days after sending that email, Maria responded:

> *Omg Shanna! I'm reading this and bawling at the same time. Thank you for sharing this with me. I'm going to add you to my prayer list and am here to help you and your husband through this. How many of these surgeries has your surgeon performed? You want someone who has done this thousands of times. I will help your husband prep for recovery too. Whatever you guys need bc this is going to be a road but if you have a good support system and lots of love all will be well! All my Love*
>
> —*Maria Menounos*

Maria was not only authentically passionate about helping me, but she also followed through. In a matter of days, she was connecting me to others who could help me on my journey through personal connections and her podcast. She even went so far as to ask us to meet with her and her husband Keven via Face-Time to talk through the mountain we were about to face and help us prepare the best we could.

After I emailed my colleagues and friends, I posted on Instagram. After posting I received countless calls, comments, and messages of support, and Dr. Amy Pittman sent me a direct message.

Amy and I had been classmates at William Jewell College, where she stood out as one of the most brilliant and funniest individuals I had ever met. Her stoic demeanor and astute observations made her humor even more surprising and on-point. As sorority sisters in Delta Zeta and members of the dance team, and our travel buddies, we had become very close friends in college. To those who know her well, she is affectionately referred to as "Pitts."

In the summer of 2000, our friendship was put to the test during a survival trip with eight other students. The last few days of our two-week journey will forever be etched in my memory. After trekking through the dense, soggy Costa Rican rainforest with heavy backpacks, rappelling down waterfalls, climbing trees, dragging our feet uphill through mud, and constructing make-shift beds from whatever resources we could find (think wet sleeping bags covered by large leaves), we were treated with an unexpected opportunity to scuba dive when we crossed over to Panama. The heat of the long days and strenuous activities had caused us all to shed some weight over the course of the experience, and we were ready to let loose.

We received a brief lesson before diving, primarily focused on proper technique, staying close to the boat, and not descending too far below the surface. Breathing techniques and the importance of ascending at a safe speed were also emphasized. In our excitement to explore the vibrant ocean life surrounding us, we listened as best as we could before eagerly jumping into the water. Two hours later, it was time to return to the boat. As I swam toward the dock, I started feeling lightheaded. Amy and I began gathering everyone's gear off the boat when I turned to her and said, "Pitts, something doesn't feel right."

She saw that my hands were spasming and cramping uncontrollably against my body. Struggling to breathe, I was losing control. Amy sprang into action and helped me sit down, immediately summoning the attention of our guides. They quickly carried me to the van while the others hopped in, and we sped off toward the nearest hospital, two hours away.

As I lay my head on Amy's lap, my hands continued to spasm and cramp. Our guides grew concerned that I had decompression sickness, also known as "the bends," a condition that can occur while ascending too quickly. Throughout the entire ordeal, Amy remained by my side, offering words of comfort and reassurance. After several tests at the hospital in Panama, it was discovered that I was anemic. It is strongly advised for people with anemia not to dive because of potential oxygen-carrying issues. This coupled with a loss of electrolytes and weight explained the muscle spasms and cramping in my body.

That night, back at our base camp, Amy and I were sleeping in our bags next to each other. "Hey Pitts, thank you for never leaving me today," I said. "I don't know what I would have done without you. That was scary."

"I was just as scared, Shanna," she responded in her monotone voice. "You know I always have your back, and I'm relieved it wasn't something more serious. Plus, don't forget that you helped get me down that mountain after a fire ant attack two nights ago. I guess, we are each other's angels."

However, I hadn't seen her since the summer after college, right before she left for medical school. All those memories came flooding back when I saw her message on Instagram:

> *Hey Shanna. I'm so sorry to hear about the acoustic, but I am glad you have a diagnosis. Who is your surgeon? Just thought I would offer a second opinion if you want or need one. Let's talk this afternoon if you can.*
> *—Pitts.*

I called Amy the day after getting her message. After our discussion, I overnighted my medical records to her office. Another instance where a connected digital health record would save time and avoid error. She shared the report with Dr. Doug Anderson and Dr. John Leonetti, cranial base surgeons with Loyola Medicine in Chicago, Illinois. At the time they received my report, they had performed nearly 2,000 surgeries specific to acoustic neuromas over a span of three decades. That's five times as many as my local surgeon. They were the experts I was searching for.

Amy called me shortly after they received the files and told me that Dr. Leonetti would like to give me an initial second opinion over the phone.

From the moment of the first hello on that call with Dr. Leonetti something clicked.

"I know without a doubt that we can help you," he said energetically. He told me they would have a different approach to my surgery, and he thought it would be worth it for me to come to Chicago and meet with him and Dr. Anderson.

This was a pivotal moment—one that I knew would have a profound impact on my life. As the brilliant Mel Robbins says in *The 5 Second Rule*, "You are one decision away from a completely different life." I felt like this decision was mine. As I posted my deeply personal story on social media, desperation for a second opinion fueled my actions. Then came Amy's unexpected response offering to introduce me to Dr. Leonetti. A spark of hope flickered inside me, shattering the oppressive darkness of silence, loneliness, and despair that had consumed me for so long. In that moment, I felt truly seen, heard, and validated—no longer lost and alone in my search for answers.

Two days after Thanksgiving, my husband and I were on a plane to Chicago for an in-person introduction and conversation with the doctors to determine whether this was my care plan. I knew that I needed to do everything in my power to get the best health care I could, and if that meant traveling away from my family and friends, I needed to do it.

As we took an Uber to Loyola for the appointment, what struck me first was how big and unfamiliar the hospital was.

Deep breath, I reminded myself.

Feeling my body stiffen, Jeff leaned over and said, "This isn't home, but it is where you're going to get the best help."

I knew he was right.

As we got out of the Uber, the driver, who had been cheerful and overly chatty the whole ride, handed us a card and said, "It's the holidays, thank you for getting a car, which gives me a job, and enjoy your trip to Chicago."

As he drove off, I opened the envelope. The Christmas card included a $1 dollar bill and a note that read: *One choice can make all the difference in someone's life. Thank you for making the difference in mine today. Blessings!*

I had tears in my eyes, and I looked at Jeff and said, "Well, he is right. One choice can make all the difference."

Jeff grabbed my hand, and we walked into the front door of the hospital.

I sat waiting in Dr. Leonetti's room, nervously twisting my green silk blouse around one finger and reminding myself to breathe. Every few minutes I would go through a cycle of reminding myself why we were here, the importance of the right care, and the outcome I wanted. I was seeking a full recovery, I had the ability and luxury to go after that, and I wasn't going to stop until I found it.

I'd lost choice and control in having this brain tumor, but what I could control is where I went for my treatment and who I trusted with my head. What I could control is who I let perform surgery on my brain. I could—and needed to—control my attitude and my outlook. I had to mindfully choose how I would respond in this moment. This was an interview, and I was hiring someone for the ultimate job—to save my life.

A moment later, Amy walked through the door and she looked the same as she did at good old William Jewell College—only now with a white coat, glasses, and the title *Dr.* before her name. I got up and threw my arms around her. She started laughing and hugged me right back.

"I am so happy you are here," she said. "I know that this is the right team for you."

Dr. Leonetti came into the room. The energy between Leonetti and Amy was incredible, and I could tell that Amy had a lot of respect for him. Dr. Leonetti asked me about myself.

I started to talk but couldn't stop the tears when I mentioned my kids.

"Listen," he said, his face serious. "There is this Tom Hanks movie that once said there is no crying in baseball. Well, the same rule applies here. There is no crying in brain surgery." And then he gave me a big grin.

We all laughed. The power of humor is magical in moments like these.

After a few minutes of discussion, he explained that the surgery he and Dr. Anderson would perform was called a translabyrinthine craniotomy, a procedure that would remove the mastoid bone and some of the inner ear bone to expose the mass of the tumor. The surgery had a greater than 90% success rate at stopping the tumor growth and removing the most possible.

He told me I would lose my hearing on my right side and there was a good chance of permanent damage to my facial nerve, resulting in paralysis of the right side of my face.

That unsettled me, and he could see it in my face.

He looked at me, put out his hands for me to put mine in his, and said, "This is going to be a big surgery with a big outcome. We are going to get that tumor out in the first and only surgery."

Dr. Leonetti stood up to leave and I rushed to hug him before he could protest. This made Amy laugh out loud, her dimples on full display. She then led me to the next appointment with Dr. Anderson and smiled the entire walk. She knew I was in the right place, and I could see how happy she was.

Jeff and I sat down in Dr. Anderson's room, which was less inviting than Dr. Leonetti's and felt a bit more like a hospital. I felt my breathing shorten again and focused on the reason we were here—to get a second opinion and decide between the hospital in Kansas City or Chicago.

Dr. Anderson came through the door. He seemed larger-than-life and had a stern appearance. He answered my specific questions about the size of the tumor, about what made this life-threatening, whether I would be able, after surgery, to be the mom I was before, and whether I would die.

Dr. Anderson looked at my husband and said, "I want you to know that the day she goes into surgery will be the longest day of your life. We will update you along the way and do everything in our power to get the tumor out."

He looked at me and said, "Shanna, you can continue to ask me questions, but what I want you to really know is that you are going to go to sleep, wake up, and get back your life."

Get back my life. No. Take back my life!

After news of my tumor, I was constantly balancing between the frightening unknown and the familiar life I once knew. The wire was thin, with infinite space beneath it.

I knew without a doubt that the surgery was going to happen at Loyola in the hands of Dr. Anderson, Dr. Leonetti, and their extended team of physicians, clinical staff, and technicians.

Health care is personal, and my very personal connection had gotten me the second opinion that was right for me. This was going to be a big surgery with an even bigger outcome.

I would get—no—I would *take* back my life.

Audacious Optimism in Action

The weight of my brain tumor diagnosis and impending surgery pressed down on me like a boulder. The sudden realization of what lay ahead was overwhelming, but it also ignited a fire within me. It gave me something concrete to focus on, a challenge to overcome. I didn't choose this diagnosis, and anyone who has embarked on a health journey knows that you can't simply run from disease. You must face it head-on.

This is true for any moment that pierces your heart, changes your environment, or redirects your path. When life plunges you into darkness—whether due to illness, loss, or unforeseen challenges—remember that resilience resides within you.

Tips on how to choose audacious optimism when life pierces your heart:

- **Don't hide from yourself:** Change often arrives uninvited, disrupting familiar landscapes. However, it's where transformation takes root. Rather than resisting, allow yourself to feel it fully with any emotion that is there. Emotions—both fear and hope and everything in between—are part of being human. Acknowledge them without judgment. Don't hide them from yourself—I promise they will surface somehow. If you have to sit in your car and cry, just cry. If you need to let out a frustrated scream, just do it. Don't hide them. Feel all those feelings and then move forward. By embracing vulnerability, you create space for resilience, healing, and adaptability.

- **Reframe change:** Change is both inevitable and profound—your darkest moments can be pivotal turning points. When faced with adversity, recognize that within the struggle lies the potential for transformation. Trust that even in the depths of difficulty, there's an opportunity for growth and renewal. Instead of viewing adversity as an obstacle, see it as a catalyst. Ask yourself: "How can this experience shape me positively?" Perhaps it's an opportunity to change old patterns, reevaluate priorities, or deepen connections. The struggle becomes a chisel, sculpting a more authentic you.

- **Let your inner voice free:** In moments of doubt and confusion, listen closely to the stirring in your gut. It's your intuition, your inner compass, guiding you toward what truly matters. Though it may have been hushed by the chaos around you, let it roar with the force of a lion. Clear your throat, raise your hand, step forward, or take any other action that physically puts you in motion to speak. Allow it to fill the room, demanding attention as you ask the tough questions and speak your truth. Remember, your inner voice is your alarm bell, your compass, your fiercest advocate.

- **Be courageous:** Embrace the alchemy of transformation and let it course through your veins. Like a piece of coal under immense pressure, your darkest moments can refine your character into a shimmering diamond. Allow discomfort to be the catalyst for growth and change, turning pain into wisdom and courage. Sometimes, the greatest leaps forward are the most frightening and in complete darkness. Summon your audacity and make bold decisions, even when they seem daunting. Whether it's seeking out a second opinion, leaving the relationship or choosing an uncharted path, have the courage to take risks and embrace the unknown. Let courage be your guide in making daring moves, as that is often where true growth and positive change occurs.

- **Envision and reach:** Close your eyes and imagine the ultimate outcome of your goals, situation, or challenge. Visualize yourself waking up after surgery feeling ready to take back your life, or getting the big job, finding the perfect relationship, starting a business, or making that bold move. Hold onto that vision with unbreakable determination. See yourself overcoming any obstacles and emerging stronger than ever before—fueled by a fierce sense of hope and possibility. Just like an athlete does before a game, visualize winning and then reach for it!

With every challenge comes the opportunity for immense growth and transformation. As you navigate through difficult circumstances, you are not just surviving; you are evolving into a stronger, more resilient version of yourself that can conquer any obstacle in your path. Choose audacious optimism, and watch yourself emerge as an unstoppable force.

Big Surgery, Big Outcome

December 2017: Let It Go

I started making plans.

I confirmed my surgery for January 11, 2018, the furthest out they would allow. This would be past Christmas and my son's birthday.

I called the hospital in Kansas City to let them know I was going with another surgical team. I thanked them for their time and care and canceled my surgery. The hospital doctors had been incredible in how they found my diagnosis and talked me through my options. They did save my life. When I called the hospital to cancel my surgery, the staff member who answered the phone said repeatedly, "I just want you to know that if you cancel with us and a few weeks after your surgery you have a problem with your head, we are not going to offer you any help."

My teeth clenched against each other, and my jaw tightened with the familiar sensation of anger bubbling up inside me. The voice on the other end of the phone sounded indifferent, treating me like a mere paying customer rather than a desperate patient in need of life-saving surgery. I fought to keep my emotions in check and maintain a sense of control. When really, all I wanted was to scream at them for their callousness and lack of empathy.

"I completely understand," I said. "And I really want to thank you and the office for your kind service."

There was no goodbye, just a click of the phone. I gave a hysterical laugh out loud and thought, *Wow! Did I ever make the right choice!* This is just more proof of why the patient experience has to change.

I started lining up care for our kids. I would need to be in the hospital for seven to 10 days and then stay in Chicago for at least a week after to heal with close monitoring. Pitts agreed—actually insisted—to take care of me in her home for that week after. She invited Jeff to stay as well, all while she was pregnant.

With so much out of my control, the few areas I could control were mindset and general health. I had been told that the healthier I was going into surgery, the better my recovery would be.

I can do that! I thought. I knew how to envision the outcome I wanted and how to pursue it. In this case, it meant training my body to be the healthiest version of me. I had been a professional athlete for the freaking NFL, and if there was one thing I could do, it was to make sure I was the epitome of health. I ran, walked, trained, ate right, meditated, prayed, and spent as much time as possible with my kids. I was going to enjoy every minute I had and be ready for surgery when it was time.

While checking off my list, organizing my life, and training my physical and mental health, I was also Christmas shopping. That year—2017—was going to be the best Christmas ever for my family, which somehow translated into buying all the gifts. Santa presented a ridiculous show of presents that year for a nearly-two-year-old and a three-year-old. That season wasn't my finest spending moment, but I knew what I was doing. I was channeling my mom.

The year my dad died, 1989, my mom made Christmas beautiful for me and my two older brothers. I will never forget the presents under the tree and the pure joy she created. I wanted that to be the memory my kids had of 2017. I didn't want them to remember this Christmas season as the one where Mom had brain surgery. In full disclosure, it was for me too. I wanted to remember a beautiful Christmas with my babies before I went into the unknown of a big surgery.

Christmas morning came early, and the kids opened their gifts and promptly passed out. Jeff and I sat on the couch drinking hot chocolate and lounged for hours. Christmas day turned into night, and soon we were carrying both kids to bed with their faces still covered in chocolate from Jonah's birthday cake that evening.

In our house on Christmas, we celebrate Jesus in the morning and Jonah in the afternoon. It is quite the day!

In bed that night, Jeff turned to me and said, "You made this day absolutely unforgettable."

I squeezed his hand and drifted off to sleep as a shadow of a thought passed through my mind—*But what if I forget it?*

The morning after Christmas, we got up with the kids, who were eager to see their new toys and books still under the tree. I made some coffee and put *Frozen* on the TV. Then I snuck away to grab some loose paper from my journal. I sat down at the kitchen table where I could see both singing and dancing to *Let It Go*, and I wrote my kids a note.

They were so small and would probably never remember this moment, and that is why I had to write them a note. When they learned to read, I wanted them to understand what Mommy went through. I knew I would share it with them at some point. I didn't know when, but I just needed to write it.

Dear Ava and Jonah,

You don't know this right now, but mommy is going to have a big surgery. I have been unhealthy for several years and the only bright spot in my life has been the two of you. You are my loves, my joy, my world, and I love you more than you will ever know. One day, we will talk about this moment in time, and I will tell you how scared I was and then how brave I became. Being brave is hard, but I remember the two of you little cuties and it becomes easy.

I hope you never remember this moment, because I will remember it enough for all of us. I hope you hear me tell the stories of this experience and think how proud you are to have me as your mom. I hope you never have to face anything like this, but if you do, I will be by your side the whole way. I hope you know I love you. I love you. I love you.

Butterfly kisses, nose kisses, and magic kisses all over your face, my babies. I am going to go get better for me, but most importantly, for you!

Mommy

I folded the note and shoved it back in my journal, wiped away the tears, and took a deep breath. I had done everything to get ready for this moment. I had checked every box I could with every ounce of optimism I had in my body. Truth be told, my insides were knotted with fear.

Every single worry, every single thing that could go wrong, and every single divergence from normalcy multiplied in my mind by the minute. I had subdued these overwhelming thoughts by concentrating on the things I could control. Now that I'd checked everything off my list, that wasn't going to work anymore.

I was scared. No, I was terrified, and I needed to wrap my mind around all the emotions spinning like a catastrophic tornado through my mind. That evening after putting the kids to bed, I went and sat on my bed and I pulled out my journal again. I had to face my fears. Really face them. I needed to write them down, no matter how hard it was to actually put that freaking pen to paper.

I am afraid of recovery and possible permanent damage.
I am afraid of something changing in my personality.
I am afraid of losing memories.
I am afraid of losing the physical ability that I have now, and not being as strong.
I am afraid of losing my face and having paralysis on the right side forever.
I am afraid for my family to lose me and not get back the same wife and mom.
I am afraid of something going wrong in surgery, or after, with an infection and the real possibility of dying.
If that were to happen, I am so afraid for my kids to lose their mom when they are so young, just like I lost my dad.

As I wrote that last line, my emotions caught in my throat. There was a fear buried deep inside me that I would live out my dad's story: fight a disease, lose the battle, and my young kids and spouse would be left to pick up the pieces of their lives. I was afraid for my kids to face life with the heart-piercing hole of a parent dying or coming back different.

My heart was heavy, my mind was exhausted, and I lay back and closed my eyes. I fell asleep with my journal on my chest. At some point that night, Jeff put it on my side table and pulled a blanket over me.

The next morning, I woke up vomiting thanks to vertigo and began crying. I mean really, really crying. Sobbing so hard that I was physically making sounds as if something were being stripped from my body. I knew it was my pain. The pain I had been denying myself to truly feel as I tried to control my health and ignore my fear rather than face it. The pain of letting go of the only version of me I had known. Letting go of the body I knew and loved to what would come *after* this moment. I didn't know that person; I didn't know what that moment would look like or who I would be.

People believe in gods of all kinds; others believe in the power within or from the universe. I have a very personal faith of my own, and that moment can only be explained as deeply spiritual.

I dropped to my knees on the bathroom floor and sobbed, pushing every emotion out of my body. In that moment, I let go of everything. My deeply buried anger. My sorrow. My family. My kids. My husband. My mom. My brothers. My extended family. My friends. My love for speaking. My ability to interact with others. My smile. My face. My career. My joy of dancing. The person I was at that moment. The person I had always been. Me.

I surrendered it all, and I let go.

In that moment I knew that whatever I got back after surgery would be the ultimate gift. I had to give up everything and accept losing it all to truly approach recovery with gratitude.

Life is fluid. It shifts course, sometimes dramatically and drastically. I had to accept this. More than that, I had to embrace it to move forward. Only when I wrapped my arms and heart and mind around the pain could I let it go. Only then could I truly see a new life on the other side.

January 2018: Redefine the Impossible

The next few weeks, I held on to Ava and Jonah tightly. I picked them up, ran around, and played with them. I would be away from them for nearly three weeks and wasn't sure how I would feel when I returned or what kind of mom I could be. I knew I wouldn't be allowed to pick them up for at least two months, and all I wanted to do was hold them.

One day, I was pretending to have tea with Ava and Jonah. Ava, then three, looked at me and then behind me, almost as if she were looking at someone else, and started giggling. I asked what was so funny because Jonah and I wanted to laugh with her over our tea too.

"Mommy," she said. "Your angel is tall."

For all our differing opinions and beliefs, the mind of a small child holds all realms of imagination and faith. I was open to all the support I could get. So I thought, *Bring on the celestial army!*

The week slipped by with a lot of smiles and laughter. I woke up on January 10, 2018, and knew that it was time to go. I checked my bag to make sure I had everything I needed: lots of pajamas, my kids' Charlie Brown blanket, a few relics to remind me of my strength and support system, including a *survivor* necklace given to me by friend and former cheerleading coach, a picture of my children to put beside my bed, and a bracelet worn by my late foundation founder and friend, Jeanne, that read, *Redefine the Impossible*.

Which was exactly what I planned to do.

I put on a "good vibes only" sweatshirt, straightened my long brown hair, and looked at it in the mirror a few more times. I knew it was going to change. My kids woke up, and I took turns holding them with my eyes shut. Then I looked into their faces, kissed their noses, held their hands, and smelled their hair. Let me tell you, there is nothing harder than walking away from your children in a moment like that.

Jonah stayed behind with Jeff's mom as Jim, Jeff's dad, drove us and my mother to the airport. Ava came with us to ride along with Grandpa in her cute polka dot pajamas.

I don't remember the car ride there, but I remember getting out and the burning in my chest as I kissed Ava goodbye. She looked at me with a worry line in her eyebrows and said, "Mommy . . . are you coming home?"

I've never had my heart torn into pieces, but that look and question sliced through every inch of my being. I looked her straight in the eyes and said, "Absolutely, baby girl. Take care of Jonah while I'm gone."

I kissed her and walked away.

We left Kansas City bound for Chicago. The sun was shining, and even with the emotional morning, I felt calm. I was ready. I just wanted to get to the other side of surgery, and I was putting my armor on for recovery.

As the plane took off, I remembered something senior pastor, Adam Hamilton, had shared. I held his words close to my heart in those weeks following the diagnosis, and I hold them close now. He said, "The worst thing is never the last thing."

Audacious Optimism in Action

There will always be factors beyond your control that test you to the very core of your resolve.

Hope, an active and powerful force, empowers you to gather the courage to confront any challenge that comes your way, while building confidence. With each step forward, you visualize overcoming life's most difficult chapters, letting go of uncontrollable outcomes, and reaching for opportunities. This not only creates space for adaptability but also strengthens your resilience to come back even stronger from setbacks.

Tips on how to choose audacious optimism to confront any challenge:

- **Understand what you can influence:** There will always be things beyond your control. However, you still have power over certain aspects such as your mindset, response, and actions. It is important to prioritize these areas and take small steps toward managing them. Ask yourself, "What can I do right now to help or improve the situation?" "What do I need to let go of?" This will lead to progress in a situation that may initially feel overwhelming, giving you a sense of control and helping you navigate through difficult times.

- **Hope is not passive:** When you let go of control over uncontrollable outcomes, you make space for hope to enter. For example, instead of struggling to hold onto a difficult relationship, you release the stress and start focusing on yourself. This allows you to see a future that may look different from what you expected. Hope is not passive; it is an active force that drives you forward. You want something better—something more. Even in uncertain times, hope gives you the strength to seek solutions, adapt, and find positive aspects. Hope does not ignore challenges; it empowers you to face them with courage.

- **Let it go:** Let go of any lingering concerns about the future and instead, focus on the present. Take a deep breath and embrace the here and now, freeing yourself from the weight of constantly worrying and controlling every possible outcome. It is important to acknowledge these potential paths, but do not let them consume you. You might even write them down and then crumple up the paper and throw it away. By releasing your grip on what may or may not happen, you open up room for opportunity that comes with change.

- **They call it a comeback:** The power of resilience shines through even the most challenging of circumstances. It is a quality born from accepting what cannot be changed, allowing one to bounce back from any setback with greater strength and determination. Like a strong tree caught in the heavy wind, resilience is the ability to bend without breaking, weathering whatever storms may come with grace and perseverance. I have even found myself at times saying quietly, "This will not break me." It is powerful when you acknowledge your own strength, and it is a true art, learned through experience and a willingness to embrace challenges and come back stronger.

- **Imagine the outcome:** Take a moment to shut your eyes and picture yourself overcoming the current challenge in your life or achieving that one goal you want to conquer. Now, keep them closed and look past that moment, allowing yourself to dream even bigger—something that may even seem impossible at first glance. The truth is, your journey doesn't end once you overcome the obstacle or achieve the goal. It will always continue, with new challenges and triumphs along the way. You must dare to imagine and have faith in the best possible outcome at every stage of your personal narrative.

As you push ahead with audacious optimism, remember that challenges will always come and setbacks will inevitably happen; expect them, and tap into your mental toughness to move forward.

CHAPTER

10

My Fight Song

The alarm sounded: 4:45 a.m., January 11, 2018. The early morning in Chicago had arrived. *Just breathe, Shanna.*

I went to the bathroom, closed the door, and looked in the mirror. I started to brush my long hair that hung far down my mid-back, almost to the end of my ribs. My hair was gorgeous, and I had never appreciated it as much as I did in that moment when I knew one side would be shaved off in just a few short hours. I choked down some tears and smiled with the thought, *If Pink can rock the half-shaved hair, then so can I!*

Jeff shouted from the bedroom, "The Uber is here." I washed my hands and walked out with a smile.

My mom gave me a big hug. "I love you, sweetie."

"I love you too, Mom," I replied, feeling a lump form in my throat. "But, hey, listen—please be strong today."

"Oh yes, I will," she assured me with a determined nod. "And you know what? I just know that everything will be fine. I feel at peace."

I smiled, admiring the strength and resilience of my mom. She had always loved me deeply, fighting tooth and nail to give me all the opportunities regardless of our difficult situation after my dad died. And now here she was, facing a situation where she had no control over the outcome—her daughter was going into brain surgery, also facing several potential complications. Yet she still managed to pull herself together amid the uncertainty.

We walked out the front door and down the porch stairs to the Uber, which looked notably rusty and gray even in the early-morning darkness. Jeff opened the door for me, and we slid into the back seat, trying to avoid the small rips in the leather. The driver quickly pulled out, and I gave Jeff an intense side eye. The smell of old smoke was all-consuming and ceiling material kept falling into my lap.

177

I leaned over to him and said very quietly, "I am having brain surgery. You couldn't have splurged on something a bit more regal?"

He gave me a grin and said, "Just trying to keep you humble . . . . it's only brain surgery."

When we arrived at the hospital, I changed into my gown, and they took me back to the operation prep room. Jeff told me he had a surprise for me. Throughout my journey leading up to the surgery, I would listen to Rachel Platten's "Fight Song" on repeat. While I worked out, cooked, cleaned house, ran errands, you name it, that song was on. There is a lyric in that song that says, "Wrecking balls inside my brain." It felt as if the song were speaking directly to me.

Jeff told me that he and Maria Menounos had shared a conversation yesterday, and she and Rachel had lunch together. Maria asked her to record a message just for me. Jeff gave me his phone with the sweet video from Rachel:

> *Hey Shanna! This is Rachel Platten. Maria told me all about you, and I am just sending you so much love and so much strength on the morning of your surgery. You are going to have an incredibly successful surgery. I am praying for you and sending you all the love in the world!*

The happy tears flowed. I had become my own cheerleader and believed that no matter what recovery looked like, I was going to be okay and become a beautiful and strong new version of me.

One of the clinicians turned to me and said, "It's time to go to sleep."

Amy held on to one hand and Jeff held on to the other, and the medicine was pushed through my IV. They asked me to count to 10.

"One, two, three . . . four . . ." I drifted off to sleep.

Hours, after hours, after hours passed.

During my surgery, the doctors were true to their word and continued to give my family updates. The surgery planned for eight hours extended to nearly 13, as the tumor consistency was more complicated than anticipated. They kept going until they had removed as much as they could with only mild damage to my facial nerve. The more they removed, the better the chance the tumor never grew back.

My mom and Jeff (along with two of his friends—also both named Jeff—who made a surprise visit from Kansas City), sat there the length of the day and well into the night. Jeff tells me he saw me before I remember seeing him.

He said when they walked him back to see me, his stomach was turning. He didn't know what to expect. He said my head was tightly bandaged from my lower right ear around my forward to the back of my head—almost like a huge white cast over my ear and the right side of my head. He tells me I mumbled something, and the ICU nurse said, "She is doing great."

He hadn't realized that he was holding his breath until that moment, but a huge sigh of relief escaped, and a weight lifted from his whole body when he saw me.

For me, time was confusing from the first moment of recovery. I drifted into consciousness and saw a clock straight in front of me. My throat ached. I needed water so badly, and then everything faded to black.

I awoke again in a different room, but my bed was on the wall. *Wait. How was my bed on the wall?* I weakly tried to reach out my left arm to see if there was ground. I wasn't actually on the wall, of course. I was experiencing the loss of equilibrium—a side effect of losing hearing in my right ear. My body was adjusting. In that moment with my bed seemingly on the wall, I let myself fade away into sleep again, hoping to escape the off-balance nightmare.

The next time I opened my eyes I was being taken some-where and heard them telling me to hold very still. Then there was that loud noise again from the machine I hated. That damn machine. I faded away again.

I woke up again and thought I saw Jeff on the floor of my room, but it wasn't my imagination. That part was apparently very real.

Before I went into surgery, I made Jeff promise me he would never leave me alone. For one, I didn't want to be in that state by myself, and secondly, I needed a health advocate with me to understand and ask questions. Jeff was on the floor because the unit was so full they didn't have an extra bed or lounge chair to put in our room. Plus, he was there after hours. My sweet hus-band fell asleep on the floor of a hospital room with only his coat for a pillow. If that isn't love (or pure exhaustion), I don't know what is.

The next time I drifted into consciousness, and the first moment I remember clearly, one of the attending clinicians was standing over me and asking me to smile. I tried with all my might, but I could barely move my cheek up on the right side. He asked me to close my eyes, I did as tightly as I could, but my right eye wouldn't shut all the way. It felt gooey. He asked me to swallow as he felt the sides of my throat. It was so hard, almost impossible.

He turned to two other people and said, "Her facial move-ments have decreased today."

That felt like a punch to my already sore gut, which reminded me that my stomach pain was a result of the procedure. They had made an incision across my stomach, right under my belly but-ton, nearly the length from my right hip bone to my left. They extracted fat cells from my stomach to use as packing in my head along with titanium mesh to repair the opening in my skull.

As these thoughts were going through my mind, my hand touched around the drainage tube and bandage across my stomach.

Jeff saw me patting that area and attempted a joke, "Well, you had brain surgery, but you also sort of got a tummy tuck."

I gave him a weak smirk on my left side.

I thought about what the clinician had said regarding my facial movement decreasing and I thought, *No*. I wanted to hold on to any movement I had, no matter how little it might be. *You are getting better*, I told myself. *You WILL heal.*

I understood the factual documentation of the process from a clinical view, but that was not the story I was going to tell myself. My will to heal was strong, and it was the fuel my body needed. I reminded myself about the moment when I fell to my knees before the surgery—*accept anything you get back as a gift and work to keep it.*

Later that night, when no one was in my room and I wasn't in a zombie state, I tried to smile, to swallow without straining, to close my right eye completely. Then I used my hand to help move my face muscles. All of it felt foreign.

On day three after surgery, I was fully aware and awake. I even got to try eating some mashed potatoes. They tasted so good. It was still a challenge to swallow, but the potatoes just slid down my throat. It was heaven on a spoon.

As I wrapped up my delicious meal of mashed potatoes and apple juice, Dr. Anderson and Dr. Leonetti stopped in to discuss my surgery outcomes and recovery, all of which Jeff had already heard. They told me some great news: 98% of my tumor was removed. The residual amount left had been too close to my brain stem to remove, but they didn't believe it would cause any problems.

They said there had been damage to my trigeminal nerve, or my fifth cranial nerve, because the tumor was wrapped around it. The tumor had stretched the nerve to the point of nearly snapping, which they knew because it was translucent in the damaged area. This caused the paralysis on the right side of my face and affected my swallowing, as well as drainage and tear production from my right eye. Dr. Leonetti said that it was too early to tell if this would be permanent and I should prepare for that possibility.

They reconfirmed that the hearing on my right side would be permanently gone. This was a result of the tumor's oversized growth, which resulted in having to cut the vestibulocochlear nerve, or the eighth cranial nerve, to remove the tumor. The eighth nerve is responsible for balance and hearing. The doctors told me that I would have to work on regaining my balance independent from support, and I would most likely experience tinnitus—a high-pitched ringing in the ear where there was hearing loss—and possible sensory overload.

I held onto Dr. Leonetti's concluding words. "Things will start to come back and feel more normal at about three months out and even more so at six months and up to a year. You are healthy, and you are going to do great in recovery."

I inhaled deeply and pushed out the air through one side of my mouth. I mumbled, "That was a lot of information."

He smiled and said, "Yes. But the bottom line is you are doing great."

When they left, I internalized all the information they shared. I had lost a lot. My hearing on my right side was gone. I had severe and most likely permanent facial paralysis. Because of this, my eye wouldn't close, I could barely swallow, and it was hard to talk. I thought to myself, *What would I truly get back?*

It may sound odd, but I didn't feel scared. I didn't feel sad. I was happy and sort of perplexed by this emotion. The fact of the matter was, I did not care about any of those things. I could think clearly, which meant my brain was working. I was *me*, and within all that loss, I had gained my life. I would see my kids again and be their mommy.

Nearly 100% of the ticking-time-bomb tumor in my head was removed. It was out of my head. The imposter was gone. I had my life back. I had my life back. *I HAD MY LIFE BACK.*

Joy spread through every part of my body.

After that, things started to come into focus for me. I was finally able to see my kids on Google Chat. The screen filled with their beautiful faces and tears welled up in my eyes. I could feel my heart beating faster and faster, as if it was about to burst out of my chest. At first, I hesitated to show them my whole face, worried that they would be scared by how different I looked now. But then Jeff took the tablet from me and pulled it back, his voice barely a whisper as he said, "They love you no matter what."

Ava, always curious and eager, asked to see the rest of Mommy's surroundings. With Jeff's help, I propped myself up a bit so she could see the full hospital bed and all the machines and wires surrounding me. Her innocent question cut through the heaviness in the room: "Mommy, what is that?"

She pointed to my left hand, which was clutching onto the medical IV pole. As I explained to her that it was giving Mommy some much-needed medicine and nutrients, a flood of memories hit me like a tidal wave. I saw my own father in a similar hospital room when I was just a child, holding onto a pole just like this one. In that moment, it felt as though time had folded in on itself, bringing me full circle to where it all began.

A few days later, I was able to take 10 steps with assistance. *Ten!*

That was a big deal when the ground was moving (at least to me), and the next day I went down the hallway and back. Even with assistance, it was something.

I saw the people I loved so dearly. Besides my husband and my sweet mom, my visitors included my amazing mother- and father-in-law, my super chill and joked-filled brother-in-law

Jeremy, some of my wonderful colleagues, who stood at the end of the bed and rubbed my feet, and my best friend Shea.

I received countless calls and text messages. Looking at my phone was a little overwhelming for my eyes. Messages were flooding in, and Jeff had to respond to texts and update my Instagram. It felt amazing to have a cheering section who wanted me to get through this moment as much as I did. I didn't have to keep my head up alone anymore. When others life you up with their optimism, it feels like flying.

On day six after surgery, I was able to leave the hospital, contingent on my remaining in Chicago at Amy's house for at least one week of monitoring. While all the Loyola staff was incredible, I could not wait to get the hell out of there!

I needed to leave and be free from the hospital room, the hard bed, and the constant beeping of machines, as well as all the bruising from the IVs. I knew the moment I left that hospital, I would truly leave the sickness, the imposter, the brain tumor behind and move on with my life.

It was time to go, and the paperwork had been done for a few hours. "Why aren't we leaving?" I asked after being patient for as long as I could.

The nurse replied, "The hospital is full, and there seems to be a shortage of wheelchairs available for your discharge and safe transportation to the car."

I told her I understood. I mean, I did. I was a liability. Until I was outside the doors of Loyola, I was their responsibility and that meant they weren't going to let me go anywhere without a wheelchair. I gave the nurse a genuine half smile and said, "I get it. Thank you so much."

When she left, I glanced at a walker in the corner of my hospital room and looked back at Jeff and his parents and thought, *Protocol be damned*. I said with as much of a smile as I could give, "Grab me that walker, because I am walking the fuck out of here."

My father-in-law let out a huge boisterous laugh. He got up before Jeff could get there and brought me the walker. He handed it to me and said, "It looks like we got our girl back, type-A attitude and all."

I pulled myself up and gave him my still weak half smile and said, "Agreed—now, let's get me one step closer to home."

Jeff and Jim flanked me on either side of the walker, and Ann stood right behind me, ready to catch me if I fell backward. I looked straight ahead as I took tiny steps and pushed the walker forward. I never looked back or down, just once to the side to give a wave to the staff at the desk on my way out. I knew they were supposed to stop me, but to their empathetic credit at that moment, they didn't.

When I was a child, I was on a T-ball team with all boys for just one short season. I showed up to every practice, played my best, and was always that girl with two braids who didn't belong on the boys' sports team. One day after practice, our coach held up the game ball that he was going to give to one of the players and said, "I am giving this to the player who every time they hit the ball and run, they look straight ahead. They don't have a single base out because they keep their eyes to the front and keep going. Now, who do you think that player is?"

All the boys started yelling, "Ryan," who was the best player on the team.

"No," the coach corrected. "It is our little smiling Shanna. All of you boys should take a lesson from her. She doesn't look back. Her eye is always on the ball or straight ahead to where she is running. She is focused, and you should all be running just like her."

As I walked the length of Loyola to my first steps in recovery, that memory came into focus and I thought to myself, *Eyes up, eyes forward, and never look back.*

Audacious Optimism in Action

In this part of my journey, when I woke up in the hospital, it felt like Christmas. I felt renewed. I also felt what had changed.

In the midst of change, pain, loss, or the closing of a chapter there lies an opportunity for renewal. Keep looking ahead, as your past is a lesson and not a prison. Focus on the future, where endless possibilities await, and draw upon your inner voice and strength to navigate this unfamiliar territory. Resilience isn't just about bouncing back; it's about using challenges as motivation to conquer new mountains. Believe in your ability to overcome, as you have already proven yourself by finding renewed life after change—and I assure you, you will. Challenge doubts, judgments, and beliefs that may impede your progress, and recognize that your hope and confidence will exceed all limitations.

Tips on how to choose audacious optimism when waking up to change:

- **Welcome renewal:** It can be difficult to see pain, hurt, challenges, change, and loss as opportunities for renewal. But trust me, they are. These experiences offer the chance to grow and redefine your life, revealing new strengths within yourself: *You will get out of bed in the morning after a breakup. You will be able to interview again after losing a big job. You will be able to love again after your loss.* Every chapter holds the opportunity of something new—embrace it.

- **Use criticism to your advantage:** When faced with someone's doubts, criticism, or judgment, don't shy away. Let it come—whether it's to your face, on social media, or whispered behind your back. Instead of feeling defeated, use it to your advantage. Criticism typically means you are doing something that someone notices—good or bad, they notice.

Channel that negativity into determination and strength. Remember, you have the power to grow beyond any assumptions or expectations.

- **Keep your eyes forward:** As humans, it is natural to reflect on the things we miss, have lost, or long for. You can't help but be drawn back to people, memories, and moments that shaped you into who you are today. But it takes a conscious effort to not let those reflections pull you or hold you back from moving forward. Instead, use them as a strong foundation to propel yourself toward your goals. Embrace every passing minute as a new opportunity for growth and progress. Like a skilled athlete, keep your focus on what lies ahead of you and run boldly and confidently into your future!

- **Remember you're a champion:** Here it is again! It's time to tap into your mental toughness and discover creative solutions while navigating unfamiliar territory. Have faith in your ability to overcome any obstacle, no matter how daunting, and envision it—envision yourself crossing the finish line, envision yourself winning. Just as you have overcome losses before, trust that you have the strength to conquer any challenge, break through any barrier, and achieve success beyond measure. Believe it with every fiber of your being, and take action toward reaching your goals and fulfilling your vision of triumph.

- **Soundtrack of courage:** Discover your personal anthem, the song that speaks to your soul. It could be "Beautiful Things" by Benson Boone, or "I Can Do It with a Broken Heart" by Taylor Swift—both are amazing songs, by the way. When self-doubt starts to creep in, turn up the volume, and let the power of music awaken your courage and motivate you to take action and believe in something greater; it's a reminder of your inner badass!

Choosing audacious optimism during life's chapter changes often feels like learning to walk again, talk again, smile again. Embrace this journey, take small steps, and trust in yourself.

CHAPTER 11

I Will

After slowly walking out of the hospital, we took a cautious car ride to Amy's house, where she lived with her husband, Dan, and their two dogs. Amy was in a surgery, and we would have the house to ourselves for a couple of hours before she got home. Once inside, Jeff walked me to the back room where Amy told us I would be staying. Leaving the hospital had been exhausting, and there was a lot of snow making the drive to her house slow. I was so happy to finally be lying down again. As my head hit the pillow, Jeff lowered the lights, and I faded off to sleep.

I woke up a few hours later to the smell of something cooking. If I haven't mentioned it yet, Jeff is an amazing cook. I was still having problems with swallowing and chewing food that was too solid, so he was making some sort of creamy soup. The smell was warm, savory, and comforting. It smelled like home.

Amy came in to check on me. She asked me a few questions and made sure I was comfortable. The biggest concerns with post-craniotomy patients are cerebrospinal fluid (CSF) leak that could lead to meningitis, brain swelling, stroke, or other infections such as sepsis. Knowing this list of concerns, I felt fortunate to be recovering under Amy's care rather than being released from the hospital to recover on my own.

After we talked, I gave her a weak smile and faded back into a short sleep. The weight of my head felt so foreign. I put my hand on my scalp, touching my scar and stitches and thought about a book I had been reading, *Cinder* by Marissa Meyer. In the book, the main character was part human and part machine after surviving a fire as a child. It's a Cinderella story with a sci-fi twist that I loved. I felt like Cinder. Maybe not quite a machine, but like someone had invaded my body, my very soul, and now part of my head was titanium.

As I sat up, I took my hand and felt from the top of my incision right by my temple all the way down the C-shape at the bottom of my neck just under my earlobe. This was a killer battle wound.

Exhaustion took over my body. It was a heavier exhaustion than I'd experienced since being alert. I felt sick, like I had a fever and muscle aches. It was hard to be in tune with my body after a surgery like that, especially with the high dose of painkillers. I knew this exhaustion was different than my healing body had felt just a few short hours before.

Amy came in to take my temperature. Sure enough, I had a fever. Now, to her professional credit, she remained calm and said she was going to give the doctors a call. She left for a short time and came back to say she was going to run to the CVS down the street and pick up a UTI testing kit.

We tested for a UTI, and it showed quickly that I had one. UTIs can be common after having a catheter in for several days. She called in an antibiotic—another marvelous perk of recovering at a physician's house.

I was proud of that moment. I had listened to my body. I trusted myself, and I spoke up quickly. In an instance like that, a UTI can turn into something much more serious if allowed to progress. Even in my groggy state, I remembered the lessons I had learned from my six-year journey and the ramifications of downplaying any symptoms. I would not make the same mistake again. I would always champion my self-knowledge and share what my body was telling me.

Amy told me later that when she left the room after taking my temperature, she had called Dr. Leonetti immediately. She was concerned that I could have been septic, an infection in the blood caused by harmful bacteria. If I had been, a very different scenario would have played out, and I was deeply thankful that wasn't the case. Within about 12 hours I was feeling back to my post-brain-surgery healing self.

Over the next few days, I started to move on my own, supporting myself on the walls. On day five of my stay at Amy's, she gave me a glass of white wine and said, "Are you ready to pull that drain out of the incision in your stomach?"

I thought she was kidding and said, "Umm . . . not here. Aren't we going to the hospital to do that?"

She smiled and said, "Sure, Hospital Pitts." Pitts was her nickname since our time in college.

She then told me to drink some of the wine. She said it wasn't going to hurt, but it would just feel funny, and the wine was for my general anxiety. I took a sip of the wine and it tasted so good.

"Go ahead," she urged. "Keep drinking a little more."

If my doctor was telling me to drink, I wasn't going to argue. I drank a bit more, and on the count of three she pulled out my drain, which felt like a long snake with a burning sensation crawling out of my abdomen. Nope, no, thank you. One and done and never again. I finished the glass of wine. I asked for another, and she said, "One is enough. Hope you enjoyed it."

I pouted. That was just mean.

I will forever look back at the six days I spent at "Hospital Pitts" with fond memories. I felt so cared for in the most fragile moment of my life. It was like being in a time machine and I was back in college with Amy, and she was saying, "I've got your back."

I truly believe there is a higher power directing who we cross paths with in life. Some people perform everyday miracles in our lives. Some give gifts we can never repay. I was meant to meet Amy at William Jewell College. We were meant to depend on each other on a survival trip in a dense rainforest, and she was meant to be there 20 years later to help me find the life-saving health care I needed.

On day seven, January 25, 2018, Dr. Leonetti and Dr. Anderson gave us clearance to leave Chicago. Jeff loaded up and helped me into the passenger seat. Amy put a traveling neck brace on me, packed me with pillows and blankets and told me not to let the pain set in because I would never get on top of it once it started. She said, "Take the pain medication. I know you want to be off them, but I am telling you an eight-hour car ride home after brain surgery is not going to be fun."

I promised her I would, and we hugged goodbye. My left eye started to water with tears, and I told Amy there was never going to be a way for me to thank her properly.

"You don't need to," she said. "You're alive, and that is good enough for me."

Eight hours later, after an agonizing car ride home, we were home. My colleague and friend had been on the babysitter rotation to watch the kids that day and night. She had gotten the house ready for our arrival and even helped Ava and Jonah make a sign that read *Welcome home mommy, we love you so much*, with their handprints all over it.

We arrived at nine o'clock that night, so she had put them to bed already. While I was excited to see them, I was exhausted and happy for the opportunity to go to bed myself and see their smiling faces in the morning. I gave Janice a very weak hug and thanked her. Then I asked Jeff to help me to our room. I didn't want to talk to her much because I felt embarrassed about not being able to use the right side of my face. That was a new feeling, and it immediately worried me how my kids would react in the morning. My confidence was wavering, and I had to remind myself to breathe.

Jeff held all the weight of my body as we walked up a long flight of stairs. On the way to our room, I peeked in on both Ava and Jonah. A rush of emotion hit me, and I felt tears rolling down the left side of my check. One of the side effects from my surgery was an inability to form tears on my right side. When I cried, tears would form on the left, and I'd get a bit of a pressure headache on the right.

I wiped my lopsided tears away, and Jeff and I continued to our room. He helped me shower and change into new pajamas. As I lay down in bed, I pulled up the covers, closed my eyes, and took a deep breath. I was home. I was home with my kids, in my own house, and in recovery. This is where I had wanted to be. This is where I needed to be. This was the beginning of my next chapter. I faded off to sleep as those thoughts settled on my healing brain.

The next morning, I woke up to the sounds of little voices in the hallway. Jeff walked hand-in-hand with Ava and Jonah toward the entrance of our room. It was the most amazing sight. I grabbed a tissue from my nightstand and wiped away the goop I'd lathered onto my right eye for moisture protection, and I slowly sat up. They both had huge smiles on their faces, and they ran over to me exclaiming, "Mommyyyyyyy!"

Jeff had asked them to be gentle, so Ava stopped short of a hug and hugged my legs, which were straight out in front of me on the bed and started to pet one of my hands. Jonah had crawled on the bed in his completely full diaper and was lying beside me with his head in my lap.

Ava stood there petting my hand like a kitty and stared up at me for several minutes. I told them both how much I loved them and missed them and asked what they did when I was gone.

"Mommy," Ava interrupted. "Why aren't you talking from this side of your mouth?" and she pointed toward my right side.

I said, "Mommy's surgery gave her a few injuries that will take several weeks to heal, but they will heal, and mommy will get stronger. Want to see the scar on my head and on my stomach?"

One of the attending nurses at Loyola had told me to tell the kids right away about the surgery and even show them my scars. This would help them understand that I wasn't going to stay hurt, and I was healing. Ava smiled and said, "Okay. I wwauvve you so much."

And she reached up her hand and touched the side of my mouth.

The next hour was food for my soul. My kids didn't care how I came back, just that I did. Jonah snuggled me, occasionally giggling when I would tickle him, and Ava chatted away, telling me what they did while I was gone. My head started to hurt really bad, and it felt heavy, but I tried my hardest to ignore it so I could spend some more time with them.

Finally, it got to a point where I didn't want to keep my eyes open anymore. Jeff came up on cue, grabbed the kids, and got them ready for the day. They were going to run errands all day and hang out at my in-laws for a bit so I could have the house to myself.

I knew they left a while later when I heard the garage close. I immediately felt anxious about being alone and let myself doze off.

I didn't sleep for long, and I woke up with a pounding headache. The house was too quiet. I got up carefully and used the walker that Jeff had placed by my bed to get to the bathroom. I was okay to walk on my own but felt groggy.

I went to the bathroom, and as I was washing my hands, I looked in the mirror. I had seen my reflection so many times before, but there was something different about that moment. In the last two weeks, recovery had been so hard—harder than anyone could have prepared me for—and it was going to continue. The person staring back at me was a stranger. I didn't recognize her split face, which moved only on one side. She had zero energy. She was frail, and half her hair was gone. That person in the mirror didn't look like me.

I felt tears forming and watched them run down my left cheek. I thought back to the moment before surgery when I had come to terms with letting everything go. I had decided then that anything I got back was a gift, including my life, whatever form it took.

I stared at myself.

And stared . . .

And stared . . .

And stared.

I don't know how long I stood there, but long enough for my face to be splotchy red and my left cheek to be tear soaked. I stood there long enough to recognize a piece of myself in that reflection, and I felt a love and kindness toward her. She was a champion.

I had to embrace this—everything about it—and I was going to have to work, to choose optimism everyday, not just wait for my healing to happen. Once again, I needed to find that North Star. When the house was quiet, and the messages stopped coming, I would become my own damn cheerleader, an active participant in my recovery, no matter how hard it was and how disconnected I felt from that person in the mirror. My family needed me, and *I needed me*.

This is what audacious optimism looks like to me.

I lay back in bed and thought that I first needed to get some relief from this headache. I didn't want to take the medication. I remembered what Maria Menounos had suggested, about how other therapies had helped her with pain control and emotional recovery. I would take any help I could get! I sent a message to one of my friends who regularly saw an acupuncturist and asked her to share the information with me. She didn't just give me the number. She took the liberty of calling her for me and asking a huge favor to get me in that day. She shared my story with the acupuncturist, who made room in her schedule. Now I just needed to get there but couldn't drive for at least another month.

My mom was already on her way over, so I texted her and asked whether she would drive me to the appointment. I slowly got out of bed, got dressed, and went down the stairs by basically sliding down the whole way on my butt. By the time my mom got there, I was lying on the couch sobbing from my one eye. That was a low point for me—the pain, the facial change, and the limited mobility was feeling greater than my optimism. All of it felt crushing in that moment. My mom walked through the door, came over to the couch, and held me.

"You already did the hardest thing," she comforted me. "You had the surgery. This will get better. You are the one who always brings the sunshine to every conversation, so let's find the sunshine now."

I sniffled away a laugh because my mom was right. I was usually the sunshine, and she was typically the moody-weather woman on the lookout for rain. I pushed myself off the couch, and she helped me to the car. As she closed the door to the passenger side, I shut my eyes and let myself relax.

Maybe bold hope was sometimes just taking one small step forward at a time.

The acupuncturist greeted me with a warm smile and a gentle hug. She immediately made me feel comfortable. She said, "I see you can't move part of your face. Hmmm . . . let's see if we can't help your body fix that!"

We chatted about my surgery and where I was in the recovery process. Then she asked me to lie on the table and close my eyes. She made sure I was comfortable and put extra padding beneath my head since I couldn't lie completely flat. The lights were off, peaceful music was playing, and I felt a calming wave rush over me.

She started to apply the needles, concentrating on pressure points in my wrist, ankles, and chest, as well as the right side of my face. I didn't feel much when she was poking the needles into my face. Acupuncture points are said to stimulate the central nervous system, releasing important chemicals to the brain. This stimulates the body's natural healing ability, both physical and emotional.

As I lay there, I could see and feel myself lying on the table, as if I were hovering just above my body and looking directly at my face. I thought about what needed to heal in my body and told myself it could be done. Yes, I was talking to myself, but I was also caring for myself in that moment.

The journey of the last several years flashed through my mind, and I started to feel empowered. An energy ran through me. Something shifted in my body as I lay on the table with needles sticking out of my face. I remembered all the work I'd done to get there, to reach that very moment.

Going to see an acupuncturist and doing something I probably never would have considered before was my first step as an active member of my healing journey. This was going to be where my story began. I was not going to sit back and hope I would improve. That was wishful thinking. I was going to be bold and confident in the outcome I wanted, and I was going to do everything in my power to get there.

When the acupuncturist was done, she helped me sit up. My headache felt lighter, as did my entire body. I felt calm and present for the first moment since the surgery. We scheduled weekly appointments, and I couldn't wait to come back.

When my mom and I got me back to the house, I grabbed a notepad and a pen and sat down to write. I first thought about what I was grateful for. I was thrilled with the outcome of the surgery, for being home, for the small movement I had in my face, for the doctors who removed the tumor, for seeing my kids, for being able to walk on my own even if I wasn't 100% yet. I smiled on my strong side as I wrote down each point of gratitude.

I turned the page of the notepad and wrote the next words: *I will.* The doctors had told me they weren't sure if I would get my facial movement back because of the size and location of my tumor and how it had damaged my nerve. Well, I was going to do everything I could to help my body, and that meant I also had to align my mindset. I had to *will* myself daily to believe in my own strength, appreciate the work I had ahead of me, and celebrate the small victories along the way.

I followed the words *I will* with a list: *I will smile with all my teeth. I will close my eye completely. I will chew on both sides of my mouth. I will regain my balance, walk straight, run and dance again. I will be a better version of me.*

When I finished, I found some tape and, with my mom's help, we walked upstairs and taped it on my bathroom mirror. Just above my sink. Each morning that week as I got up, I read that note out loud. I read it even when I didn't want to. I was willing myself to recover as I looked at my image in the mirror. I read it and I *believed it*! I believed that I would do all those things.

Each day as I read that note, I would start by trying to smile at myself. Then I'd try to open and close my right eye all the way and wink at myself, which always made me laugh. Yes, something about the act of smiling and winking at myself brought me instant joy.

I would move my mouth from side to side and open it as wide as I could. I'd use my hands and move my face into a smile, a frown, and then push my eye up into an excited face. My daily face exercises helped remind my face what to do. I did that every day for a week, which turned into two weeks and then three and so on.

During this time, I also started to walk on the treadmill. I would hold on to the bars and walk slowly at first, turning my head from side to side to change my point of view. Then I started to pick up my speed. Once I was walking quickly inside, I moved outside. I used a cane the first few times just to get my bearings on the sidewalk and street terrain. On the third day, I went without one and trusted myself. I walked with a smile. I walked with my eyes straight ahead. I walked with pride in every step. I walked envisioning myself winning a race. I would only listen to uplifting music and picture myself doing things I wasn't yet able to do, such as running, dancing, picking up my kids, and speaking clearly with both sides of my mouth. I felt like Forrest Gump, walking until one day I ran.

Every morning, I began my routine by reading the note of motivation I had written for myself. With determination and focus, I completed my daily face exercises and carefully documented my progress with pictures. Each snapshot was sent to Amy and Dr. Leonetti, whose enthusiastic responses only added fuel to my determination: "Unbelievable," "Amazing," "This really is incredible, Shanna."

In just six weeks, the doctors marveled at the miraculous rejuvenation of my facial nerves. I was my own cheerleader, pushing myself to be active in my recovery and embracing an audacious form of optimism. For me, optimism was not just a state of mind and something that came on the good days, but it became an active choice. It was choosing to believe in the possibility of progress and success despite setbacks, challenges, and changes.

When I returned to work after seven weeks, I was welcomed back by my coworkers, who had adorned my office walls with hundreds of inspirational sayings and quotes. Among them, one quote from Melinda Gates resonated with me the most: "Optimism isn't a belief that things will automatically get better; it's a conviction that we can make things better." And that is exactly what I had done—I had made my recovery better through sheer determination. I accepted the challenge, the change, and made the decision to champion myself.

Eight weeks out of surgery, Jeff and I ran in the Kansas City St. Patrick's Day 5K race. The race where we'd met just five years earlier. It seemed fitting that it became the starting line for a new chapter in our lives. When we finished the race, Jeff re-created the moment when he asked me on our first date. Leaning against the bar at Kelly's in Westport with the traditional victory beer he said, "Hey there, I have been wanting to ask you out."

"Oh, is that right?" I said with my classic side eye.

"Yes," he said. "And just so you know, I will show you the world, which really means two babies and a brain tumor. You in?"

"The brain tumor isn't exactly a selling point, but the babies and the baby-making sound nice," I said.

Nine weeks after surgery, I stood on stage to represent the Kansas City Chiefs at the 2018 Cheerleader Auditions—a role I had routinely held for several years since my retirement in 2011. I had convinced myself that they would replace me that year based on what I had undergone and the fact that I was still visibly in recovery. However, my former coach and friend took me out for lunch and asked me to come back. I was floored that she, and the Chiefs, would still want me on the stage. I couldn't speak clearly because I couldn't move one side of my mouth. I tried to convince her that she didn't want me as the emcee, but she insisted, "No, you are the only one we want." She has always been a true champion for people. The one pushing the hardest and cheering the loudest when someone succeeds. I had been on her team for years, and at that moment she was my cheerleader.

She won the discussion, and I couldn't wait to get up on that stage.

When the evening arrived, I stood behind the stage curtain and felt the rush of emotion that only comes from being in front of an audience. I took one moment to be abundantly grateful for my ability to talk—even if it wasn't clear. The way I talked wasn't what mattered. What I said and how I connected with the audience to represent something I loved—Chiefs cheerleading—is what mattered.

I asked one of my fellow alumni cheerleaders and closest friends, Lindsay, to help me walk up the side stairs that led to the stage. It was my first night in heels, and I was not about to trip in front of a few hundred Chiefs fans. I wrapped my arm around hers and took my first step toward the curtain entrance. My right foot slipped, and I had to grip Lindsay's arm to regain balance. My heart pounded.

She stopped me from walking forward for a split second and said, "I got you, girl, and you got this!" She let go of my arm, and I walked out on the stage and down the catwalk one very slow, intentional step at a time.

I gave the crowd a big smile that hit both sides of my mouth. Almost. I took a quick glance stage right and saw my friends Krissy and Mallorie at the DJ booth cheering me on. Then I saw Jeff with both Ava and Jonah there to support me, yelling, "Go Mommy!"

I blew them a quick kiss and turned toward the audience.

"Good evening, I am Shanna Adamic, and I will be your host for this incredible night. I cheered for the Chiefs from the years of 2003 to 2011. I may not be on the sidelines any longer, but I am still a cheerleader for the Chiefs! And when I am not cheering for our hometown team, I am a passionate leader in global philanthropy and health care transformation. I am a wife. I am a mom to two crazy toddlers . . . and I am a proud brain tumor survivor."

Audacious Optimism in Action

As you tackle one big, formidable chapter, sometimes it seems to multiply before your eyes. Each new development brings its own opportunities, challenges, setbacks, and, my favorite, comebacks! You are no stranger to this, because you have faced the worst and emerged. Now it is time to tap into your unrelenting determination as you press on through your unique journey. Keep your eyes fixed on the North Star—bold hope—and let it guide you through the darkness with courage. And even when you stumble and fall, pick yourself up again and again and again, fueled by your will to persevere.

Tips on how to choose audacious optimism as you build your momentum to move forward:

- **I will, I will, I WILL:** You are declaring your future out loud, solidifying a promise to yourself, and speaking it into existence by saying, "I will." And for those who struggle with projecting confidence outwardly, simply create a daily representation—whether it's a vision board, journal, or even just a mental image—that embodies your vision for the future. By saying or seeing your goals and intentions, you will strengthen your commitment and not only stay on course but also achieve the desired outcome.

- **Bring on the cheerleaders:** Allow your people to be your cheerleaders by being unapologetically yourself, even during difficult times. Let the people in your life—your team, tribe, squad—see and embrace all aspects of who you are, both good and bad. They are your community of love and support; they want to cheer you on. Personally, I am always carrying a set of poms to do just that! When they witness your progress, they will celebrate your accomplishments. They will offer encouragement during setbacks which most likely will come, so put your cheerleaders into formation!

- **Grant yourself grace:** The journey of recovery (of any kind), growth, and overcoming setbacks can be arduous. It takes great strength to pick yourself up and keep moving forward. Take a moment to acknowledge and celebrate your efforts—maybe just with that smile at yourself in the mirror—for your effort is the testament to your resilience. You have endured challenges and come out stronger on the other side. Be kind to yourself, and give yourself grace as you continue on your path, just as you would for someone else. You deserve your own grace. Keep pushing forward, for every day is an opportunity for growth and transformation.

- **Step out of your comfort zone:** Take a leap out of your comfort zone and challenge yourself to try something completely unfamiliar. It's funny, because I wrote this while traveling solo on an 18-hour flight to Australia, a trip that tested me a bit. Even when my anxiety threatened to hold me back, I chose to let my curiosity guide me and boarded the plane. Real growth happens when we push past our self-imposed limitations. This could mean exploring a new interest, becoming proficient in a difficult skill, or questioning our firmly held beliefs. Embrace the discomfort and open yourself up to new possibilities you never thought achievable.

- **Bold choices:** Make a conscious effort to be daring, even if it's just one bold move a day (shout-out to Shanna Hocking). That bold move for you may be simply getting in the workout clothes for the gym, because you have a goal to be in the best health of your life this year. When making choices, choose audacity over hesitation. Be brave in chasing your aspirations, standing up for yourself, and making bold moves toward your vision or something more. Set big goals, plan small steps, and take calculated risks. Embrace failure as a learning experience and stepping stone to success. Adapt and continue moving forward no matter what setbacks come your way.

With audacious optimism as your guiding light, embrace your true self, share your ideas, take daring actions, and wear your scars with pride. Be audacious and believe in yourself and bring your whole self to every situation. Don't lose momentum!

Beautiful Brain

January 2019: The Machine

My road to recovery in the first year was filled with twists, turns, and steep hills. I remember the day I looked in the mirror and saw my smile for the first time in months. It took my breath away. I had worked so hard just for the corner of my mouth to turn up in a universal expression of joy. That small little movement was one of the greatest gifts.

The doctors requested an MRI at my one-year mark and every year after until I'd had four. On January 11, 2019, I walked into my one-year MRI in a facility in Kansas City.

I was shaking. I could barely breathe, and it took everything in me not to burst into tears as I filled out the paperwork. I realized that I had trauma, and the machine I was about to see again was the trigger.

I changed into my gown, took a few deep breaths, told myself I could do this, and walked out of the dressing room to meet the technologist. The closer we got, the more my mind and body wanted to stop walking, but I kept putting one foot in front of the other. When we got to the room, she led me to the machine and helped me lie down. She placed the familiar guard over my face and encouraged me to lie as still as possible. She gave my hand an encouraging squeeze.

As they inserted me into the tube, my whole body quaked, and my teeth clenched. My friend's husband, Zach, was one of the attending radiologists.

He got on the microphone while I was in the MRI with my eyes tightly closed and said, "Shanna, it's Zach, you are doing great. Just keep holding still and think about how quickly this will be over."

Zach and I had a unique connection because his mom had been diagnosed with my same tumor nearly 18 years before. She had also undergone an intense surgery that lasted almost 20 hours.

They had completely severed her facial nerve to get to the tumor, which was common during the earlier surgeries. As a result, she had permanent paralysis on one side of her face. She would talk and smile the best she could from one side. The few times I had met her, I remember seeing a warrior. She was deeply grateful for the facial mobility she had.

This experience made Zach uniquely compassionate in my situation, and his voice through the MRI machine kept me from tearing off that face guard and running out of the room.

When the MRI was done, Zach came into the room and helped me sit up. I was a mess. Tears were streaming down one side of my face, and I was trying to slow down my breathing. He gave me a big hug and said, "I am really glad you called and asked if I could be here. This is scary. One year out is a big deal, and guess what! You did it! Now you just need to wait on confirmation from the doctor that everything looks good."

I knew Zach would know the outcome of the MRI first since he would be evaluating it and giving the report to the doctors in Chicago. However, he had to allow the doctors to provide me with the information. So I had to wait. Maybe one day, maybe four. I went back to work and I tried hard to think about anything except the outcome of the MRI.

I sat in my office, looked at the framed picture on my wall of Rachel Platten's "Fight Song," and thought about what a year it had been. I had come so far. I could close my eye, smile with all my teeth, say most of my words clearly, chew on both sides of my mouth, swallow without being afraid of choking, and run for miles. I felt like a stronger version of myself. My one weakness was that machine.

I shouldn't be triggered by that machine, I chided myself.

Yes, it was terrifying and brought me back to the moment I heard the scariest words of my life: *you have a brain tumor*. But it also saved my life.

The greatest gift in any health journey is getting a diagnosis—the right diagnosis, and in my case, one that had treatment options. That machine helped me end a six-year hunt for an answer. The machine was the first step toward getting the right care and identifying the problem before it was too late. That machine was a gift.

As I stared off into space, thinking through all these memories and emotions, my cell rang. It had been only two hours since my MRI, so I was stunned to see Zach's name across the screen. I closed my eyes, took a deep breath, and answered.

"Hi. Why are you calling me so soon? Is there something bad? I thought the doctors would call."

"Listen, I know you are sitting there anxious, and that's why I am calling. I cannot tell you what I saw on that MRI. But I want you to know, I have seen a lot of scans like yours, tumors your size and type. You should know that you had damn good doctors."

I couldn't help but smile. I felt a tear slide down the left side of my cheek. He didn't tell me I was fine, but he told me something great. One day later, I was in a meeting with a few of my colleagues and got another call. The area code was from Chicago. I let out a very loud breath and excused myself from the meeting.

I answered the phone and said, "This is Shanna."

It was Dr. Leonetti. "How do you feel?"

I told him how I was doing and rambled on a bit, feeling my voice shake while I was nervously trying to make small talk, afraid of what he might say.

Then he said the words I'd been waiting to hear. "Your scan looked perfect. In fact, it looked like the residual amount that was too close to your brain stem to remove has decreased in size. We thought we had removed about 98% and now it looks like about 99%."

I started to cry happy tears while he kept talking. "Your brain looks beautiful. Go get another MRI at the same time next year, and we will talk again soon."

I hung up the phone and walked outside to get some fresh cold winter air and feel the sunshine on my face. I closed my eyes and pointed my face toward the sun.

I smiled, grateful to feel the tears roll down just the left side of my cheek.

January 2022: Strong Side

Why is this the hardest workout I do all day? I thought as I aggressively yanked my sports bra over my head. I mean, the struggle of getting off a well-fitting sports bra is real. There is not one woman in the world who does not breathe a sigh of relief once she wriggles it over her head. Finally, mine was off, and I was slipping on the light-blue dotted medical gown. I wrapped it around my body once, making it a dress instead of a robe.

I glanced at my reflection and snapped a mirror selfie complete with a peace sign; something I would pocket and post later to celebrate and share this milestone. *Maybe in May, around brain tumor awareness month*, I thought.

I was having my four-year MRI today, and if this scan came out clean with no brain tumor growth, then I wouldn't have to have a scan again for another three years. Since my surgery in January of 2018, I had one MRI per year every January. And every January I had to dig deep to find the strength to go through with it. *What would the machine reveal this time?* was the typical thought that ran unleashed through my mind. As the years went by, my ability to manage the fear got stronger.

Today, I was once and for all going to make peace with *the machine*. As I walked into the familiar clean white room, I heard its powerful humming before I saw the huge beast in the center of the big open space. I paused at the doorway. *How familiar this moment is.* I would say it was like seeing an old friend, but that would be a stretch. It was more like seeing a mysterious soothsayer at a circus who was about to tell me my future, eliciting both intrigue and fear.

I turned to the technologist. "Will you do me a favor?" I asked.

"And what's that?" she said with a smile.

"Can you take my picture sitting on the MRI machine bed?" She looked at me with a question on her face and I continued, "Today is a big day for me. It is also a story I want to share with others. This machine is terrifying, and I want to start telling this story differently. This isn't something to fear—it is something to embrace. I really feel like it offered me a second chance at life. So really, this machine saved my life. I want others to see that perspective as well."

The technologist gave a caring smile and said, "I love that so much. It is hard sometimes being the one to take people to this room. I see the sadness and, honestly, I can't help but feel it too at times." She went on to take the picture but told me she would need to check with the public relations staff member to make sure it was okay for me to publicly share.

I handed her my phone I'd kept hidden to my side. She looked at it and said, "You do know you can't bring that into the room, right?"

"Yes," I said with a big cheesy smile. "I was just hoping you would say yes to my photo op, so I risked bringing it with me."

I made my way to the MRI bed while she stood at the doorway, making sure to not bring the phone inside a magnetically charged area. I propped myself up and, just for the smallest moment, a familiar buzz ran through my body covering me in goose bumps. It was the same feeling I had when I sat on my dad's bed in the VA hospital a few days before he died, when I pulled the microphone earbud out of my ear on stage at the Royals fan event, when the world stopped spinning after my first episode of vertigo, when I looked right into the eyes of that bear on the mountain, when I was diagnosed. That familiar buzz of pain, fear, time-stopping moments.

The body never forgets, even if life moves on.

As I propped myself on the MRI machine, the buzz moved through me, and I breathed. *Not anymore, I reminded myself.*

I crossed my ankles and gave my best smile as the nurse snapped a few shots. She told me she would hold on to my phone during the scan. She went and dropped it off in the viewing room and came back to help me adjust on the bed. As she closed the guard over my face, I let out a long breath.

If someone would have told me a decade ago that I would be a brain tumor survivor, I wouldn't have believed them. This process taught me so much about trusting myself, embracing the unknown, and leaning on my mental toughness. It taught me to champion my own story—to be my own and very best cheerleader.

I had always been strong, but the journey had refined the conscious way I choose optimism daily. It brought back my trust in my inner voice and taught me to be an active participant in the opportunities that come from every challenge. This MRI machine had been that broken street lamp, showing me my North Star—my diagnosis, where I, again, found the power of choosing optimism. Its guiding light showed me how to regain my strength, trust in myself, and find the confidence to pursue the right life-saving health care for me.

I smiled to myself under the guard. I was in the MRI tube where no one could see me, but I could feel it. I knew right then, surrounded by the machine, that I was smiling. I made it.

The machine turned on. The loud hum started to circle back and forth overhead. I lay perfectly still, and I began to imagine. I envisioned a new sound—something that sounded equally powerful that brought instant comfort. The sound of the attic fan that embodied my childhood. I thought of those warm summer nights, hearing the lawn mowers in my neighborhood, smelling homemade hamburgers cooking, and seeing my dad on the backyard deck standing over the grill—complete with a tank top, brown skin, and a huge smile. The sound reminded me of my brother Erik going in and out of the house as loudly as he possibly could and seeing my other brother Steven circling the living room listening to his favorite music. The sound was my mom baking cookies at dusk with the kitchen window open and the summer breeze sucked in by the attic fan. The sound was family, comfort, love. I loved that sound.

And I had learned to love this one as well. The MRI's powerful hum continued, picking up to a pulsating beat.

"Shanna, what do you hope happens?" I remember my friend Elaine asking me a few weeks before my surgery.

"I hope I have a full recovery and am stronger on the other side of it."

She nodded. "Let me tell you something. Hope doesn't mean wishful thinking. It means belief. So when you say you *hope* something will happen, you better wholeheartedly believe it will, because I do. I believe you will be stronger on the other side. And I believe in your *already* strong side."

A tear ran from my left eye. My right eye still had no extra moisture to form tears, but I was okay with that. Funny enough, my left side isn't my strong side, as I had thought it would be coming out of the surgery. My right side is the strong one. The side that fought the battle, has the scars, feels the nerves that have crossed signals to confuse my facial cues, can't hear a sound, feels vibration, and has shaking muscles and a lazy eye when I'm tired. That is my strong side. That is where my optimism was challenged and triumphed.

"Just a few more minutes, Shanna," the technologist's voice came through the machine. "I'll come in and add the contrast now, and that will be the last part."

The last part. *Breathe.*

I stayed completely still and felt gratitude flow over me. My story turned out differently than so many others who get a terminal diagnosis, didn't get their diagnosis in time, or didn't have the ability or financial means to find the health care they deserved. I had the connections, knowledge, and resources to tackle my diagnosis. Just being in this machine was a privilege that saved my life.

That should be everyone's story, I thought to myself.

The thought instantly reminded me to respond to a direct message I had received that morning. It was from a 26-year-old woman in Cape Town, South Africa. She had reached out to tell me she had watched my YouTube video from the Acoustic Neuroma Association. "Your video was the first I watched when I got diagnosed with my AN. I am scared shitless for my surgery, but watching you made me feel so hopeful and happy."

This was one of several direct messages I'd received with this kind of message. *Hopeful,* I repeated. That is what I wanted everyone to feel.

A year after my surgery, members of the foundation helped me record and share my story. I didn't know how it would connect to our work yet, but I knew it would help someone, and it did. Over the past few years, it has been watched over 10,000 times and hundreds of people have reached out to me to share their journey and ask for support. I have tried my hardest to respond to everyone; I remember clearly how the response from Maria Menounos gave me the boost of confidence I needed, and I want to do that for others. I want to become their—your—biggest cheerleader.

The humming stopped. The machine turned off, and the bed started to slide backward. The technologist took out the IV, removed the guard, and helped me sit up. "You did great," she said.

I jumped off the bed, walked toward the door, and didn't look back at that machine. I had to wait a few days for my results from Dr. Leonetti's office, and this time, that was okay.

She handed me my phone and led me back to my room to change back into my clothes. She stopped and said, "They were fine with you using a picture and just asked that you tag us or send us a copy of the post. And, hey. Thanks for your smile today. This job isn't easy."

"Of course, and I know it's not. I appreciate you," I said with a big smile.

I got dressed quickly, slipping on my wedding ring as the final step. I looked in the mirror to make sure I was ready to walk out and stopped for a moment. I stared and I smiled. My smile was just a bit crooked, to me. I'm sure others probably don't even notice. I looked at the woman in the mirror and felt so proud of her and her journey that continues today.

I smiled at myself in the mirror—yes, I really did—a big one too.

I walked out of the imaging building toward my car. It was cold that January day, and the sun was shining. I couldn't help but smile as I sat in the driver's seat. I blasted the heat and shot Pitts a quick text before driving home: my fourth and hopefully final (for a while) MRI is done!

Audacious Optimism in Action

This story is not just mine. It is for:

The patient who yearns to be heard.

The patient struggling to find their own voice.

The patient fighting to find the right medicine, surgery, or cure that will save their life.

The patient who shares their story to inspire change.

The person who refuses to be defeated.

The person who fails and continues to show up again and again.

The person who believes in themselves, their voice, their ideas, and their value.

The person who chooses bold hope again and again and again.

This is *your* epic story, filled with bold and daring chapters. Be fiercely self-aware and make mindful choices that will shape your journey to live with audacious optimism. Trust in the wisdom of your inner voice—let it be your guide as you navigate the unknown with insatiable curiosity. Let your mental toughness shine, and speak your future into existence starting with the words "I will." Have faith in yourself and all that you are capable of achieving. I believe in you, my fellow optimist, and I cannot wait to see where your story takes you!

Afterword

A udacious optimism pulses through my veins. It is a life-sustaining energy. It is not just a fleeting feeling of hope, but a powerful choice that I make every day. It is a strategy for living, a way of being in the world.

My approach to optimism is not passive or timid. It is audacious, bold, and unrelenting. It is not a personality trait. It is a choice, and one of determination and confidence—inhaling all the fear and doubt that surrounds me and exhaling wild resolve and belief in myself.

At its core, optimism is an act of self-trust to embrace the unknown and accept change and challenges with determination to approach them as opportunities. For me, it also means harnessing my mental toughness and taking action to move forward, no matter how daunting the task may seem—ignited by saying, "I will." This simple declaration carries immense power, signaling a commitment to myself to boldly step into a future that I create for myself. And when I reach those goals and dreams that once felt impossible, I won't stop there. I'll keep moving forward, constantly striving for more growth and success.

By starting with a mindful choice, trusting yourself, embracing the unknown, and tapping into your mental toughness, you have the ability to create meaningful change in your own life—redefining the impossible. (Thank you, Jeanne, for teaching me this.)

My personal journey of faith, dance, love, and health has led me to become an audacious optimist in all aspects of my life—as a mother, wife, leader, and changemaker. Audacious optimism is woven throughout my story and deeply rooted in my passion for intelligent health care.

I am audaciously optimistic about the future of health care. With the maturation of AI technology, I believe we are entering a new chapter that will transform patient care for the better— from early diagnoses to quality of care to access to care. And most importantly, I believe that AI will bring clinicians back, present in the exam room with their patients, fixing a system burdened by noise.

Health care is personal. We have all been or will be patients at some point in our lives. I never imagined undergoing brain surgery or watching my father succumb to cancer, nor did I anticipate losing a dear friend to our country's heartbreakingly high maternal mortality rate. But through my personal experiences, I am driven to advocate for change and help shape a better future for many people and causes, including health care. Optimism may seem elusive in the face of such loss, but it can still be found. It shines through the cracks of grief and pain, offering a glimmer of hope to carry on, to continue living and finding happiness once again.

Audacious optimism is the guiding light through life's labyrinth, illuminating the path ahead. It is not merely a passive stance; rather, it is a deliberate choice—an audacious leap into the unknown, fueled by confidence and a relentless belief in the extraordinary.

In this you find joy—happiness—in unexpected places. It's the laughter shared with a stranger, the awe at a sunrise surrounding a stadium, the warmth of a friend's hand during life's darkest hours. Happiness may be a fleeting visitor, but audacious optimism can be a constant companion on your life journey.

This is an audacious way of living—to believe that you can choose your path, your outcome, your response. But audacity alone is not enough. It's audacity coupled with purpose—the audacity to channel our grief, trials, and losses into a force for change. We transform pain into purpose, loss into legacy. Our scars become battle badges, reminding us of our resilience.

Audacious optimists become advocates.

We champion causes, challenge norms, and rally for justice. We don't merely survive; we thrive, leaving no stone unturned in our pursuit of a better world.

In the grand stage of life, audacious optimism is the North Star. It propels you toward opportunity, urging you to seize it with both hands. By doing this, you become the architect of your own story, weaving dreams into reality beginning with a mindful choice, trusting yourself, embracing the unknown, and tapping into mental toughness

My fellow optimist: never leave behind your audacity. For boldness is not reckless—it's the courage to rewrite your story, one audacious chapter at a time.

My journey continues, as a wife, mom, leader, and so much more, and I tap into my audacious optimism daily!

I hope you are smiling. I am smiling at you!

Special Mention of the Acoustic Neuroma Association

The Acoustic Neuroma Association is the premier resource to the acoustic neuroma community, informing, educating, and supporting those affected by an acoustic neuroma, also called a vestibular schwannoma.

Their mission is to work tirelessly every day through communication, innovation, research, and partnerships throughout the medical community to improve the lives of acoustic neuroma patients and their families.

www.anausa.org

Thank you for your important work! #ANWarrior

Acknowledgments

Here we go! Buckle up because my list is long. My life has not been a solo journey, and there are a great many people to thank for merely blessing me with their presence! I am going to try to just stick to the individuals who have supported this writing journey, my health journey, and my passion for living out audacious optimism.

These notes of gratitude below come in no particular order! I realize I could never give a speech at the Oscars!

Jeff, Ava, and Jonah, my life would not be complete without you. I love you so much and when I wrote this book, I wrote it for you—you are my world. Jeff, thank you for showing me the world as you promised. I love you forever and patrostous (our secret word), my babies.

Maria, I can't thank you enough for the kindness you showed me through my health journey. You taught me to share my story to inspire others and inspire change, and you set the example for how to be the CEO of my own health. You are a rock star, a blessing, and a force in this world!

Amy, there are not enough words for you to even begin to say thank you. You saved my life. I love you forever.

Senior Pastor Adam Hamilton, thank you so much for being the inspiring communicator of God's love that you are. I have clung to your words—your faith continues to inspire me and my family.

Mother, Mom, Mommy, thanks to you and your guidance, I did not look directly at the sun ever and I am not blind! I love you. You have been the best mom.

My Hilt, Stotts, and Rice Clan—Steven, Sariah, Erik, Sheree, Aunt Dottie, Uncle Jim, Amanda, Aunt Lois, Uncle Chuck, Kristen, Patrick, Jessica, and all my amazing cousins I didn't mention—I love you unconditionally too! I feel so blessed every day by God for this crew.

LDS Church, thank you for taking care of my family and for all the kindness and community you have shared with us and many others.

My Adamic+ Clan—Jim, Ann, Jamie, Melissa, Jeremy, Madeline, Ashley, Joe, Unc, Shannon, and all the nieces and nephews—I love you unconditionally! I can hear Jim calling me a "type A" just like him, and I proudly raise my hand in agreement. Amanda and Aunt Dottie, thank you for the help on Chapter 2, xoxo.

Laura-dog and Shea-dog, no, I will never let you live down our club name. D.O.G.—Depend on God. I am laughing as I write this, yet it still is a great reminder. I have loved living life with you both. We are stuck with each other, and I love you endlessly.

Jeff and Kayce, Jeff and Maggie, Kevin and Amy, you all were meant to be in my life. I love each of you so dearly and am obsessed with our friendship that would have happened even without the Jeffs and Kevin. Amy, thank you for introducing me to my husband. Kayce, I am not sure how I would live without our friendship—Napa forever. Maggie, you led the way . . . thank you for giving me the confidence to write.

Josh and Kristi, big love for you both. Josh, thank you for being the first call and the person to calm me down.

Melissa, Amy, Francie, Tammy, and Jan, I will never be able to repay your kindness for showing up for me in Chicago. Rubbing my feet and even before that just supporting me. Or just showing up for me when I needed you most during recovery. **Melissa,** thank you for taking a chance on me early on, for your guidance, and for honestly being my second mom—I love you dearly.

Dr. Leonetti and Dr. Anderson, you gave me back my life—plain and simple! You are amazing.

Doctors and Clinical Staff at the clinic, you all always treated me with such kindness even in moments where I was frustrated. Thank you for working to try and find the answers with me. Health care is not perfect for the patient or providers, but it is filled with incredible people.

Aubree and Tori, the best nannies in the world. Thank you for living in our chaos and loving our family.

Molly, for just being Molly and going with me to Chicago to see Amy in 2022, which led to the beginning of this whole book journey. From England to the firepit with Pitts and her chickens, I got big love for you girl.

My OneCause RAISE crew, you know who you are! I love you all so much, and thank you for giving me a voice when I was finding out how to tell this story.

The Wiley publishing crew and Shanna Hocking, thank you, thank you, thank you for taking a chance on me! Cheryl, you are an amazing human. Shanna, I am so happy we share the same name, and I appreciate you so much!

Mollie, where do I begin, girl! You have been my ride or die. Literally, we have lived through some THINGS! You are the salt to my sunshine, and I freaking love you forever for it.

Natalie, I have always said that I think the universe keeps bringing us together. I have big love for your heart and share your passion for health care.

Oracle Health Foundation, Cerner Charitable Foundation, First Hand Foundation past and present team members, you are my heart and soul! You all are some of the most brilliant and dedicated people I know. Thank you, thank you, thank you! Special shout out to **Kate** and **Adam,** as you both helped me many times with pieces of this process—thank you, thank you, thank you!

Tricia, you have always believed in me. Your friendship means the world to me. Sometimes you are the mom I need, other times the aunt or nagging sister, and most times it is just the best friend. Love you!

My Oracle and Cerner work people, you are all magic. I wish I could name every single person—I feel so blessed by each of you! I will never forget my number—associate 8910!

Cat and Marc, what in this world would I do without you. You all have been my friends through literally every phase of my life since I turned 21. I love your whole family so much and can't imagine my life without the two of you in it!

Cristen and Chad, thank you for being you! There is nowhere I would rather be than on your driveway for hours. I love you both so much and am so thankful for you in this time of my life.

My Chiefs family! The Hunt Family, thank you for giving me the best years of my life representing your team! Tavia, I am giving you a big hug. You epitomize grace, determination, and optimism. I love you and your entire family!

Judah, you have changed my life in so many ways. I am thankful every day for you, my friend. You have always been my biggest cheerleader, and I will always be yours!

Mal, Lindsay, Jeron, Liz, Kerri, Lauren, and all your spouses too, what would I do without you!! I love you all! We have truly lived life together!

Ashley, I don't even know what I would do without you. You are one of the biggest blessings of friendship in my life! I love you! From the Masquerade, to every crazy golf tournament, to the whirlwind of life, we have been there for each other. You are forever stuck with me!

Jacque, Felisha, Eliza, Katie, Tiffany, Brett, Melissa, and so many others I formed bonds with through the years that stemmed from cheerleading and went far beyond—I love you fiercely.

Elaine, you will forever hold a special place in my heart as a mentor, leader, friend, and pastor. You taught me so much about faith, grace, and love. You and **Nanette** mean the world to me, and you will always have a special place in my heart.

The Patterson/Lillig Family and April, thank you for your support through the years and giving me a dose of honesty and perspective when it was needed and caring support during personal moments. Thank you all.

Cliff, your thoughtful conversation and time were precious to me during some of the most transformative years in my career and life. Thank you for being you and your ability to think big and out of the box and pushing me to think that way too!

Matt, Dan, Allan, Lynn, Ed, I couldn't have gotten through the last few years without your guidance, laughs, and golf tournaments. You owe me happy hour.

Kelly and Tarver, thank you for spending so much time with me to help me sculpt my stage presentation. You both are amazing, and I appreciate you!

My d.School and Hatch friends, thank you for helping me get out of my comfort zone and think big! Big hug to my buddy **Kirk**!

William Jewell College family, you gave me so much. My education, my foundation to try and try again, you are where I experienced love and an institute I will always love. Thank you!

Carmen, thank you for giving me the courage to keep writing very early on!

Chelsea, Jason (and Aaron), Norma, Katie, Rachel (Hollyday Med Spa), and so many more. You are all my health, beauty, and wellness support crew who keeps me put together. You know why, and you know how! Thank you!

The authors I have so dearly loved—Mel Robbins, I am high fiving you. I love you and your spirit for action. 5,4,3,2,1—thank you! Matthew McConaughey and *Green Lights*, wow, just, wow! Adam Grant—need I say more? Simon Sinek, the *king* of optimistic leadership—you are everything. And so many other experts. I love and cherish your creative and inspirational work!

I have saved the hardest one for last . . . Krissy.

My beautiful friend **Krystal (Cunningham) Anderson,** with her warm smile and infectious laughter, had become septic after complications during her second pregnancy—another beautiful life lost too soon. We bonded over our shared love for the Kansas City Chiefs, worked tirelessly together at transforming health care at Cerner and then at Oracle, and taught each other valuable lessons about optimism and standing up for what we believe in.

I told you about this book at our last dinner together on March 7 at a Greek restaurant called Paros in Overland Park, Kansas. You turned to me with that sassy look and said, "I better be in it, Shannnnna."

Krissy was a true embodiment of magic, and I have no doubt that her powerful story will ignite the much-needed radical changes in health care worldwide. Thank you, **Clayton**, for being her knight in shining armor even as she looks upon us from Heaven with your babies, James Charles and Charlotte Willow. You are a warrior, Clayton. You have been to the depths of the impossible, and you have found hope—you have chosen optimism each time you share her story.

Thank you, Krissy, for being in my life. We weren't ready for you to leave, but God called you back. The last text you sent me said, "I can't wait to meet my baby girl." I know without a doubt you are with your babies now and smiling at all of us who are holding you close in our hearts.

We love you forever.

shinewithjoy.com

About the Author

Shanna Adamic embodies audacious optimism as a way of life. As an executive leader for Oracle, she has dedicated over two decades to leading corporate philanthropy, social impact, and community engagement at the intersection of health care and technology. Her optimism fuels her personal drive for a healthier, more equitable world—where intelligent and connected health care is a reality.

Shanna's story transcends professional accomplishments; it's a testament to the indomitable human spirit.

Her journey took an unexpected turn when she faced a rare, benign yet life-threatening brain tumor diagnosis. Now partially deaf, but with an unyielding spirit, she emerged a survivor. As a result of this experience, Shanna's health journey became a source of strength, refining her optimism, fueling her drive to help others, and deepening her commitment to the change needed in health care.

Shanna possesses an extraordinary gift—the ability to unite hearts and minds under a shared vision. Whether addressing a packed auditorium or engaging in intimate conversations, her words resonate. She is a seasoned speaker and inspiring storyteller, infusing her talks with contagious enthusiasm and unwavering belief in humanity's potential.

Shanna is also a former NFL cheerleader for the Kansas City Chiefs and was a proud athlete for the organization for eight seasons. Now, as an international speaker and published author, she channels her energy into storytelling to ignite hope and spark change.

In a world often clouded by doubt and cynicism, Shanna Adamic stands tall—as an inspiring example of audacious optimism. Her story reminds us that adversity can be a catalyst for transformation, and that even the darkest moments carry within an ember of hope. As Shanna shares her very personal walk through life, cheerleading, and her health journey, she invites us all to embrace audacious optimism—which begins with a mindful choice, trusting yourself, embracing the unknown, and mental toughness.

Index